THE RIE™ MANUAL:
FOR PARENTS AND PROFESSIONALS

MAGDA GERBER
EDITOR

Published by

Resources for Infant Educarers™

1550 Murray Circle, Los Angeles, California 90026

To order additional copies see Appendix "F"

RIE Manual

The RIE MANUAL: FOR PARENTS AND PROFESSIONALS
Edited by Magda Gerber
Published by:

Resources for Infant Educarers ™

1550 Murray Circle, Los Angeles, CA 90026
phone 323-663-5330 • fax 323-663-5586
Home Page: www.RIE.org   Email: Educarer@RIE.org

Cataloging-in Publication Data provided by Publisher
The RIE manual: for parents and professionals /
edited by Magda Gerber -- Los Angeles, CA :
Resources for Infant Educarers, 1979.

143 p. : ill ; 28 cm.

Includes bibliographic references.

   pt. 1. Practical suggestions for parents. -- pt. 2. A philosophical bridge from Hungary to the United
States. Reflections upon my work with Dr. Pikler; The Loczy model of infant care; Have infants been cared
for with respect?; What is appropriate "Curriculum" for infants and toddlers?; From stress to distress /
Magda Gerber; Notes on theDemonstration Infant Program / Phyllis Sletten; Suggestions for language
development / Ann Davidson. -- pt. 3. From Hungary. A quarter of a century of observing infants in a
residential center; Can infant/child care center promote optimal development?; Forms of hospitalism in
our days / Emmi Pikler; Developmental schedules stimulating adult education attitudes; The importance
of person-oriented adult/child relationships and basic conditions thereto / Dr. Judith Falk; Examination
of the social contacts of infants and young children reared together; Feelings as one of the main scenes of
the adult/child relationship / Maria Vincze.

  ISBN 1-892560-00-3 (pbk.)

  1. Infants--care. 2. Infants--care--Hungary. 3. Child rearing. 4.Infants--Health and hygiene.
  I. Gerber, Magda. II. Pikler, Emmi. III. Resources for Infant Educarers (RIE).

  RJ61.M36 1979

  649.122 --dc21

TABLE OF CONTENTS

PART I: PRACTICAL SUGGESTIONS FOR PARENTS

**PART II: A PHILOSOPHICAL BRIDGE FROM HUNGARY
TO THE UNITED STATES**

PREFACE

This collection of papers describes a special way of seeing and caring for infants. It is of value to all people concerned with infant care, including parents, infant carers, educators, physicians, therapists, those who implement day care programs, as well as those who advise or consult with parents.

The collection begins with practical suggestions for parents. Some of these articles are based on actual conversations between Magda Gerber and Cara Wilson, a mother of two sons. Ms. Wilson participated in an infant/parent guidance class led by Magda Gerber and was so enthusiastic about the help she received that she wanted to share the insights she gained with others. This led her to write a regular column in <u>After Birth</u>, a newsletter for parents of infants, featuring articles by and dialogues with Magda Gerber.

Sections of Magda Gerber's writings and teachings are included in Part II. Magda Gerber studied and worked in Hungary with Dr. Emmi Pikler. Magda Gerber has used the Pikler philosophy and methodology in her work with parents of infants and in her training programs for professionals in infant care. In her innovative programs and her lectures, she describes the application of the "Loczy" model to American culture. Resources for Infant Educarers was founded to incorporate and disseminate this philosophy, referred to as the RIE approach.

The third part begins with speeches and articles by Emmi Pikler M.D. who directed the National Methodological Institute for Residential Nurseries* in Budapest, Hungary. Part III continues with papers by various members of Dr. Pikler's staff. When editing these articles we did not include extensive bibliographies, we used only selective references.

For simplicity's sake we refer to the infant as "he" and to the parent as "she" throughout this collection. It is hoped that the conventions of our language structure will be outweighed by the advantages of clear reading.

RIE wishes to acknowledge the Board of Directors and the support and expertise of the following persons: Phil Marsh, editing; Elizabeth Memel, desktop publishing; Eileen Gerber, RIE logo design and original art.

---

*After Dr. Pikler's death in 1984, renamed the Emmi Pikler National Methodological Institute for Residential Nurseries.

PART I:

PRACTICAL SUGGESTIONS FOR PARENTS

Articles by and Conversations with Magda Gerber excerpted from Cara Wilson's column in <u>AFTER BIRTH</u>, a newsletter for parents.

ONE POINT OF VIEW

Cara Wilson

The key word in Magda Gerber's philosophy is RESPECT...respect for your baby and respect for yourself, the parent. An awareness of your child's point of view, as well as your own, will greatly help in building a respectful relationship. Such a relationship will be reciprocal — the child's nature will reflect back the love and respectful handling and attention he has received. Magda's approach involves a heightened awareness of the subtleties in the daily caring routines of an infant-parent relationship.

When you pick up your baby, first tell him what you plan to do. And when you want to put him down, tell him that, too. Simple! But how often people grab babies and plop them down like they were little dolls — loveable, but emptyheaded. Talk to your child as if you are having a conversation with him. Help him to feel he has a thinking, feeling part of whatever you are doing to him and for him. Magda talks to children with such dignity. She treats them all, from infants to toddlers, with such respect. Respect for the child is the key to understanding Magda's philosophy. What happens when you respect someone is that you put a little distance between yourselves. That distance sets the two of you apart from each other, so that you can see each other more clearly.

Allow the child to experience conflicts and let him be active in them. Any problem that the child can handle by himself is good. Let him take the initiative as much as possible. For example, Magda moves the box where Daniel's truck has rolled. She doesn't hand him the truck. She lets him discover where it is, he sees it behind the box, crawls over to it, feels proud that he found it. With an older child, you direct him in a questioning way so that he can solve the problem by himself, thus learning to trust his own ability. It's not "There's the ball over there." Instead say "Where is the ball? Do you think it's over there? Where do you think it is?" Include him in the problem and in the solution.

The crying child is not instantly retrieved (if it's obviously not an emergency), but rather the mother remains calmly and peacefully in the child's view, her face not a mirror of his pain, but with an expression of strength and solace. The crying child crawls or walks over to mother. She lets him experience pain or sorrow without grabbing it away from him, and he is allowed to choose when he wants her comfort.

Try to hold back as much as possible before intervening with two fighting children. When you must help, try not to interpret their feelings. You verbally reflect what you see. Reflect. Magda uses that word a lot. It's really another form of keeping your distance and seeing things more clearly. Avoid imposing your opinions or emotions. When the fighting involves two angry children (old enough to understand and respond to verbalization) both pulling at the same toy, you simply restate the conflict as you see it. "I see you both want that toy. Steve, you want it. Paul, you want it too." By stating the problem and not imposing any value judgements, you give both children the feeling that you really understand where they're at. All the time you are speaking with the "aggressor" you are being gentle to him. If it made you furious to see him biting or pulling hair or beating on the other child, let him know it, but don't bombard his aggression with your own aggression. Any angry response by you would simply reinforce or teach more aggression. At the same time you are gently calming the "aggressor" you are equally calming the "victim." Don't overdo your sympathy to him. Let him know you are sorry he's unhappy, see that he's not hurt anywhere and get him back on his feet. Too much sympathy and fussing over a "victim" makes him enjoy being victimized. This gentle approach to handling a screaming "fur-flying" moment works on babies, too. They might not understand all the words, but by saying "gentle-gentle" and stroking those poking, pinching, pulling little hands, the message gets through. Your peaceful attitude calms things down. By physically being gentle, the child learns what gentle means.

Choices should be in a child's life as much as possible, but they must be true choices. "Cheese or apple with juice?" is a true choice. You are prepared to give him what he wants. A false choice is "Would you like to go to the market now?" when you know your child has to go with you. He doesn't really have a choice, and that's deception.

Orders can be very good. Give the child simple, uncomplicated, direct statements. "I don't want you to go outside the gate." No long explanations are necessary. Simple "I" orders expressing your desires are enough for the child and easy to understand.

Food: Give the child less than what he wants so he'll ask for more. This way he can ask several times more for food and he will be eating as much as he wants, not as much as you want. Always keep a positive approach to food. Don't urge him to eat more than he wants. He should not be made to feel that he is eating to please you. This "ask-for-more" approach satisfies both the child and parent. The child feels totally in control of what he wants to eat and you, his parent, are pleased with his requests. You are helping him to enjoy food and the whole ritual of mealtime, and he's making you happy.

ON LOVING

If one were to list all the cruelties and maltreatments, both physical and emotional, that parents and adults inflict on children under the guise of love, the list would be a long one. But, going beyond such sinister examples, even kissing and hugging may or may not convey to a child that he is loved.

Love is a feeling, an emotional state. Artists, writers, philosophers, poets have tried to define it. Marcel Proust says, "Love is space and time measured by the heart." What is space and time? It is the here and now. It is you.

As unfortunately I am no poet, I will try to recall from my own experience how it feels to be truly loved by someone. It makes me feel good, it opens me up, it gives me strength, I feel less vulnerable, less lonely, less helpless, less confused, more honest, more rich; it fills me with hope, trust, creative energy and it refuels me.

How do I perceive the other person who gives me these feelings? As honest, as one who sees and accepts me for what I really am, who objectively responds without being critical, whose authenticity and values I respect and who respects mine, who is available when needed, who listens and hears, who looks and sees me, who shares herself—who cares. Cares. To care is to put love in action. The way we care for our babies is then how they experience our love.

How and when we   pick them up

smile at them

talk to them

hug and kiss them

tolerate their crying

set limits

restrain

allow frustration

allow free exploration

allow free choices

foster independence

give clear messages of how we feel
and what we expect

To come back to spoiling, as this word also has many meanings, I will now use it to mean not spoiling the child (by making him a brat) but spoiling his capacity to cope with life.

In the name of love --
We can "spoil" by overprotecting ("don't do this,"
"be careful," watch out," "don't touch").

> *Real care is to take the time and create a safe environment in which the infant can safely explore, and the mother and father can relax.*

We can "spoil" by controlling ("do this now," "take this toy"). Many prescribed baby-stimulating projects advise us to do just that.

> *Real care is using the time we naturally spend with our babies, to learn, teach, experience together what is happening.*

We can "spoil" by constantly entertaining, thus taking away their natural curiosity and capacity to entertain themselves. Boredom is not in a young child's repertoire in an adequate environment. We can easily condition a child to be bored, by over-indulging, doing things for him. This is faster and easier.

> *Real care is to allow the time, have the patience and encourage even the youngest baby to do whatever he is capable of doing for himself.*

Ask yourself what your baby means to you?

- a plaything with whom you can play dollhouse?

- a helpless creature who makes you feel omnipotent?

- a puppet you can make dance to your tune?

- a love object who gives you sensuous pleasure?

- a pet who wags his tail when you praise him?

- an extension of yourself who will fulfill your thwarted goals in life?

Of course there is a little of all of these in all of us.

If my rumination on love leaves you more puzzled than reassured, here is a guideline: the combination of love-care-respect. Lucky is the child who grows up with parents who basically accept and love themselves (read Erich Fromm's The Art of Loving to understand that this does not mean selfish love) and therefore can accept and love their child, who reminds them so often of their own selves.

Crying, sniffling, wailing, weeping...what's a cry anyway? What does it mean when our children begin their lives with a cry? What's good and not so good about our children's tears? We all have a need for some kind of sane answer, some sort of guideline to lean on when we hear our young people wailing. I brought our questions to Magda.

Q. Magda, so many parents want to know why babies cry and what they can do about it when they do cry. What would you tell them?

A. What I do tell parents really depends on the age of the baby and on many other circumstances, but I would include the following: All healthy babies cry. We would worry if they didn't cry — no infant can be raised without crying. To follow the advice "Don't let your baby cry" is practically impossible. At times the harder a mother or father tries to stop the baby's crying, the more anxious they become. Both parent and baby end up "crying together," making a helpless couple. Watching any angry crying baby with a bewildered mother or father, I often wonder who is more helpless.

Q. But why do infants cry?

A. The immature organism has to adapt to dramatic internal and external changes. Think of the adapation it takes for a man to leave the earth and go to the moon. Then think of the changes an infant experiences and has to adapt to when the child leaves the womb and enters our world.

According to scientific studies most crying occurs between 4 and 8 weeks of age. This crying happens regardless of how the parents respond to the crying. Speculation is that the baby spends the first weeks in a state of drowsiness and gradually becomes aware of the environment impinging on him. We believe that newborn and very young infants cry when they feel discomfort from:

1. Hunger.

2. Pain (could be gas, irritated skin, etc.)

3. Feeling too cold or too warm.

4. Sudden changes in position (equilibrium off-balance).

5. Sometimes a change from wakefulness to sleep and vice versa are vulnerable transitional times. Picking up a child has an alerting affect, so it is terribly hard for a sleepy, crying child jolted into the vertical position to once again try to sleep. Sometimes just letting the little one cry those extra parent-painful minutes before sleep can be crucial. Some children seem to really need to cry themselves to sleep.

6. Too much stimuli from environment (noise, light, activity) around the child. An often-repeated belief is that babies cry when bored. Actually, they cry when <u>over</u>-stimulated.

   Also, contrary to common belief, babies do not cry when wet. They do cry, however, when they have a diaper rash which is irritated by a wet diaper or when the wet diaper causes them to feel cold.

   A very young baby may cry to discharge energy.

   Though there is a great variety of crying right from birth (and I'm pleased that Dr. Leboyer, <u>Birth Without Violence</u>, does not believe this has to be eliminated), as the baby grows the crying becomes more differentiated, more expressive crying. It becomes a form of communication.

Q. What seems to be the common reaction by parents to the child's cry?

A. What different parents do seems to be greatly influenced by their beliefs (what they read or are told by "experts") and by their own needs. The parent who likes to eat would feed the baby often; the parent who feels too cold or hot will cover or undress the baby; the compulsively clean parents will change diapers frequently. Responding to rapidly shifting trends, parents will pick up, jostle, carry around and rock their babies. The way a parent responds to the baby "conditions," the baby expects specific responses (feeding, covering, rocking). Instead of responding to real need, the parent responds to a created need...conditioned by the parent. The wider the parent's repertoire, the more varied will be the baby's responses.

Q. Magda, what does all this crying do to the parent?

A. All kinds of things. People react in different ways at different times, each in their own ways. It's really interesting. And crying triggers off all kinds of reactions.

   It may:

   alarm the parent.

   arouse feelings of being more needed than ever before. This feeling can be a very gratifying one, almost giving a powerful feeling of omnipotence, as if the parent were a magician who can change an unhappy child into a happy one.

In contrast to this reaction is almost the complete opposite in the way of: great helplessness, bewilderment, frustration and often anger. Crying can change a concerned parent into a battering parent. Or to use a milder example, just watch the way the pacifier is thrust into a baby's mouth. The message is "shut up."

Q. Do you have any advice for us, Magda?

A. Parents need to try and change their thinking. Do not want to stop the crying. Respect the child's right to express feelings, or moods, whether crying or smiling. Try to find and eliminate discomfort. What will determine the baby's feelings of trust are the security in the child's daily life and the anticipation of a predictable rhythm. If the child's life is very hectic and unpredictable, then the only secure base is the parent. However, the next important task for an infant is to achieve some autonomy or the capacity to feel secure even without the parent.

No, it is not only what you do when the baby cries, but what you do all the time the child does not cry. This makes the difference between sensitive and less sensitive parenting.

Q. But Magda, you still did not tell what you would do when a baby cries.

A. I would ask the baby why he cries.

Q. A three month-old baby?

A. Yes. A child, no matter what age, will respond to your focused attention, your calm voice... these will eventually reassure the young person. The child will learn to give better cues and you will learn to understand him better. This is how dialogue between infant and parent develops.

To quote Sidonie Greenburg (author of The Wonderful Story of How You Were Born, and co-author of The Many Lives of Modern Woman) "Just as the smiles and gurgles and small sounds of satisfaction are infant language, crying is too."

DISCIPLINE

Close your eyes and mentally clarify how you feel about discipline. Open your eyes and write down your own definition of it. You may be surprised as I was after reading this dictionary definition of discipline: "Training that develops self-control, character." The root of the word is "disciple," which means to follow an examplar.

If one would think of what is to be accomplished, what is to be achieved by discipline, there would be an entirely different feeling for what it is. With discipline, you must have a certain goal in mind. Basically, most parents are afraid of disciplining their children because they are afraid of the power struggle. They are afraid of over-powering the child, afraid they will destroy the child's free will and personality. This is a terribly erroneous attitude. A positive goal to strive for when disciplining would be to work at wanting to have children we not only love, but in whose company we love being. Lack of discipline is not kindness, it is neglect. Sometimes it is very difficult and even painful to discipline. It is easier to say, "Yes, okay, have your own way." But then what has been accomplished?

Confusion over discipline arises when you lose sight of what is important and what isn't. I will refer to discipline as the Red, Yellow, and Green Light. I'll explain. The Red Light is when the baby crawls on the floor right over to a big, sharp knife. Watching this, you don't stop to ponder about the effect grabbing the knife away will have on the child's psyche, you just cleanly reach and pick up the knife or the child. With "Red Light" there are no guilt-weighing, ambivalent thoughts. You just do what you must do immediately.

With the Yellow Light the situation can be negotiated. For example, the child wants you to be with him at the moment you want to do something else. Should you sacrifice your moment for the child's demands or is that not realistic just then? Again, we go back to knowing what is important at the time; not just for the child, but for you, too. It helps to be strongly attuned to your own inner rhythm — to know what your needs are, and to convey this to your family so they learn to respect your needs too. When you give yourself the same respect you give your children, that teaches the children respect for you also. Sacrificing you own needs for the child's only creates inward anger within both of you. If it is important that you finish reading the newspaper before you play with your little person, then clearly convey that message. Let the child know what it is you want to do for yourself and what you expect the child to do, so that playing quietly while you read can later grow into hours of secure separateness; both of you doing something independent of the other and still feeling good about your relationship.

The Green Light is when you want what the child wants. You give the child a few choices of something to do and you are ready to do any of them. We all need many green lights in life to be able to accept the reds and yellows, too.

It is not always easy for parents to say "No." A parent's ambivalances, guilt feelings and areas of confusion in his or her role will be picked up and used amazingly fast by children. They seem to have a sixth sense for it. Any ambivalence from a parent will produce a nagging response. Know what it is that is important, both for you and for the child. If you are not clear, the child's nagging will persist, which will make you, the parent, even angrier. This in turn highlights the conflict that exists already, leading to an unhappy situation combining anger, guilt and fear.

When parents feel guilty because of anger at the child, the anger-guilt becomes a distorted, dishonest message. When you "please-whine" at your children and promise them something, anything, if they'll only listen to you, you are unconsciously creating guilt in them. When the parent becomes pleading, sticky-kind and guilt-sweet, this creates guilt in the child and eventually fear. Guilt because the child's anger is being whined-away by the parent, making the child feel too powerful. The child is forced to internalize aggression that should be externalized and dealt with openly by the parent. It also creates fear that the parent is not really in control and is not being honest. The child knows when the reaction doesn't fit the situation. Be Clear. Be Honest.

I prefer giving acknowledgements, rather than rewards. Do not promise a reward for behavior that you can expect of your children, let them know how good you feel about them. Just seeing the beaming smile of admiration on his parent's face is reward enough. The commonly used "good girl", "good boy" often becomes mechanical and is sublty demeaning. It implies a child's value as a person is contingent on his behavior. It can create a conflict for the child. He may think he is "bad" if he acts differently than what he has just been praised "good". They don't need big hooplas, just a strong acknowledgement on your part that they did a good job.

Children need expectations. They need to know where they stand in all kinds of life situations. They need to know the rules. Discipline is an integral part of this rooted, secure feeling. From birth on, the parent sets the life-space for the child. An ambivalent parent will make things more difficult. Know your role as a parent. You must have certain goals and principles for your children.

One misconception most parents share is that children must be happy all the time. That is an unrealistic expectation because there are instinctual desires we all have but can't obtain at that moment, or maybe ever. Life is a combination of pain and pleasure. Young children cry when they can't have what they want. Parents so identify with the child and the tears that they can't bear not giving them their heart's desire. But it is not the best thing to try to keep your children happy all the time. That is not the way life is. Many goals involve pain to get there. That is the human condition. When children find this out too late in life, after being sheltered and buffered unrealistically, they will find things difficult and frightening to cope with. There is no way over-indulged children are going to be happy, because they seldom get direct honest responses from their parents. These parents are basically negligent. Children are begging for discipline and for structure. A child has a difficult time growing up with ambivalent parents. When you say "No", really mean it. Let your face and posture reflect "No" as well.

Once the external disciplinary lessons are learned, the child begins to internalize — to learn the lessons on his own, and even realize that some things that are desired are not always good for us or for the others. Structure, expectations, predictability — all add to responsibly raising and loving our children. The freedom we all feel deep within ourselves comes once we understand where we stand in the scheme of things.

TOYS

Many parents are concerned about the how's, why's and what's of toys. Toys should be sturdy but simple. I do not like busy toys. I like busy children manipulating their toys in many imaginative ways. Balls of all sizes, boxes big and small, wooden boxes and stepstools to climb on and off of, kitchen utensils, pots and pans, stacking toys, containers that objects can be dropped in or out of, open and close toys, dolls, picture books, pull and push toys, cars, and of course, water, sand and a climbing/playing area in which to experience the toys.

When you are trying to decide whether any object or a toy is appropriate, you may test each object using some of our guidelines for free play. The environment should be:

1. Safe.

2. Have enough space for the baby to move freely.

3. Include objects that are safe and simple. These objects should be basic, able to be manipulated in many ways and not requiring adult help or supervision. They should require the child to be active, not passive. They should also be cleanable, show variations in size, weight and shape, and embody different functions (e.g., containers, push and pull toys, role play toys, etc.) The arrangement of objects should be orderly, and the furnishings should be geared to the child re: scale, placement, etc.

As far as educational books and toys, I feel that the best thing to teach a young baby is everyday life. 1) About his needs: "Are you thirsty?" 2) About his belongings: "Where is your shirt?" 3) About your concerns: "Where are my keys?" "The food is hot." Babies have to learn the most important things in life — who they are, how to communicate, what makes mommy and daddy happy or angry. Teach them about yourselves, and they will learn about themselves.

The mother of a three-month boy: "I clean house and set him up in his infant seat and take him from room to room with me. However, he still gets fussy and I feel guilty for cleaning instead of playing with him. Am I letting him demand too much of me?"

This mother's problem represents the trap I feel too many mothers fall into, the trap created by books and advisors who say that a baby needs to have his mother near him at all times. As a result mothers keep their babies on kitchen tables, bathroom floors and other unsafe places. To keep them safe, they are strapped in infant seats, where they can hardly move. Children learn best through involvement, both with their environment and with others. All a confined baby can do is kick his legs while his mother works. But if the child could have a pleasant place to play, where he could move around on his own, exploring his environment, and, in turn, freeing his mother to do her own work, both mother and child's needs could be met. A baby can learn to spend time by himself. It is important for him to discover satisfaction and joy in his own independence. And, when the mother finishes with her own time, she can come back to her child and be able to fully concentrate on interacting with him without distraction. No infant needs constant attention; what he needs is to feel secure. Certainly being shuffled from room to room is not security inducing. An adult way of life is not a child's way of life; and when adults try to do their own work while trying to pay attention to their children, both parent and child end up feeling frustrated. Both need time for themselves. It will help make the together times all the more rich.

Teaching is not a separate function. It is an everyday life experience. (Read How Children Learn and How Children Fail, by John Holt.) Too many educators put pressure on parents to try to teach their infants earlier and earlier. What should infants really learn? If the parents are always telling the child what they are doing, the baby is learning about the real world around him. A safe environment in which the baby can move and explore is the kind of learning experience the child profits from the most. Teaching is one thing and learning is another. What the parents teach is themselves, as models of what is human, by their moods, their reactions, their facial expressions and actions. These are real things they need to be aware of, and of how they affect the child.

QUALITY TIME

Quality Time! We all talk about it. We all want it, both for our children and for ourselves. But do we really know what it is all about?

It is full, unhurried attention. Under the right circumstances it is a peaceful, rewarding time for <u>both</u> parties because, ideally, it's a time of no ambivalence, one for open listening, taking in the other person, trying to fully understand the other's point of view. This unique time can happen under many circumstances, but I divide it into two themes:

1. The "<u>Wants Nothing</u>" Quality Time. That's when the parent doesn't want to do anything with the child, has no plans other than wanting to simply be with the child. Just floor-sitting, being available, being there with all the senses awakened to the child; watching, listening, thinking of only that child. It sounds easy, but few can truly do it.

Most of us are used and conditioned to <u>doing</u> something. This is not "I've-got-to-do-this" kind of time. It's more a time for taking in and waiting. We fully accept the child's beingness just by our own receptive beingness. We are telling the child that we are really there and aware. <u>Not</u> what shall I cook, clean, whom to call, etc. If you really feel that you should do something during this time, then it's not the right time. This is a free-flowing space in which the child shouldn't feel he has to perform, because the parent is not sending out the kind of demanding messages that say, "I am here now, what would you like to do?" Most relationships are based on performance. We tend to stimulate our children to produce listening and watching. If the child seems to ignore you and is doing something completely on his own, don't leave. It is very comforting to know that the parent is there, really <u>there</u> without the little person under pressure to have to do something to keep the parent's attention.

For an infant it's a peaceful presence — a quiet assurance in this beingness. This separate play from the parent teaches the child to depend on his own inner security. If you do this with a newborn, you learn to see the child fully, you really observe and discover a person unfolding. This separate time doesn't produce immediate results. Please remember this. <u>Everything</u>, especially new things, need time and patience. You must plant and then reap. First put in what you feel is right and then slowly it takes. This instant, ready-made society expects instant results. Not so with quality time. It's more like an investment in the future of your child as well as in the present. You are available, waiting; the child is the initiator.

2. Also, there is the "<u>Wants Something</u>" Quality Time. This is when you <u>do</u> have a goal to accomplish something together, such as dressing, bathing, feeding, etc. This too should be regarded as quality time. You can make sure the child knows that this time is different from your "Wants Nothing Time" by actually saying "Now I want to diaper you." "Now it's time to get dressed," etc.

This is a time when you work for cooperation. If you think in terms of quality, you use the time for learning to do a task together when you expect the child to cooperate. It should become something you both enjoy doing together. Your <u>availability</u> is still there, except that during this time you also have <u>expectations</u>. This is the beginning of introducing and reinforcing discipline.

Around age two, a child's most important task is to become autonomous. Before this time, you and the child have what is called a "symbiotic" relationship — the parent and child are almost like one. They depend emotionally on each other, and, from this attachment, both eventually have to separate from each other. This is the separation-individualization stage, when the child becomes an individual. This takes a long time and during this separation phase the child will try his wings out by teasing, challenging and gameplaying.

There are two attitudes that are helpful in dealing with these games. (1) You enjoy and acknowledge this playfulness. But when it's time to get down to business you are (2) FIRM. You allow a little time to play the game and you let the child know you are playing, then you become firm and say it's time NOW. You don't back off — you don't reverse your message. "We really have to get dressed. We've played, but now it's time. Can you do it yourself, or shall I do it?" Now we are not playing games with the child because we want to get the job done. Try not to get angry. Be matter-of-fact and not aggressive. Anger only excites the child to want to play more. You don't respond to silly business at this stage. The play is over. "I would have liked to do it together, but now I have to do it for you. Maybe you can still help. Here, pull this up." Fooling around is very much part of development, but the child does have to cooperate later; I'LL DANCE WITH YOU AND THEN YOU MUST DANCE WITH ME.

Quality time is a time of growth, movement, ebb and flow. If you can give these two kinds of quality time ("Wants Nothing" and "Wants Something" themes), then you are really growing with your children. It's the consistency of the time you are giving that does so much. Don't worry if you can't get together every day; the rhythm of your togetherness won't be broken. It's what is happening consistently that counts, not mechanically. You can be together hour after hour in great <u>quantities</u> but not actually connect, see, hear or respond to each other. That's not what quality time is all about, for the beauty of this special kind of availability is how it affects the older child and later the adult who was raised with it. You'll find that they never feel they have to be forced to talk. They can peacefully sit with the parent and then open up when they want to. The child never feels manipulated. What you do with your child is an investment for the future. Quality time is what everybody really wants — a gift of time and attention.

OUTDOORS

I always tell parents how much easier they could raise healthy, "happy" children if they would make outdoor living a regular habit for your babies. Why? Because babies thrive out-of-doors. They sleep better, eat better, look better, play better and learn better. Fresh air (though I realize "fresh air" is becoming staler each day) both soothes and stimulates. So, an ideal situation would be to live in a fairly smog-free area with direct access to a fenced-in yard with grass and trees. Make the best investment and buy (easily available secondhand) a duplicate crib and a playpen.

Q. Why couldn't parents just take their baby out in their arms or carry a portable crib outside each time?

A. In my experience, when you have to carry out a crib or playpen every day, several times a day, it just gets to be too much. Like most activities in daily life with baby, whatever gets done regularly and routinely gives predictability and security to both baby and mother.

Q. At what age should we start this "habit?"

A. A healthy full-term newborn can be taken out at about 4 weeks of age. At first, only when the temperature outside is similar to the one in the child's room. Keep the child dressed or covered the same way he is indoors. Keep the crib in the shade and take the child out preferably after feeding and diapering. Most probably the child will fall asleep. After about 15 minutes the first time, you can increase the timing so rapidly that in a few days the child can spend longer hours, eventually the whole day outdoors. At first, the very young babies will sleep much of the time, but as they grow older, they learn to enjoy doing outdoors the same thing they would do indoors (sleep, eat, play).

Q. All this confined in a crib?

A. Certainly not. When a baby becomes 3 months or older, most of the waking hours are spent in a playpen. Ideally, the child should have a very large playpen (small room size) in which to roll, crawl and eventually creep. After 12-18 months, a small part (large size room) of the yard should be fenced around and eventually a safe, fenced-in yard will become the child's territory. All playpens should have a bottom part made of wood, a firm pad covered with plastic and a cotton cover on top, tied to the bars of the playpen. It is not pleasant to have a naked body in direct contact with plastic.

Q. Should babies stay outdoors in both summer and winter?

A. It doesn't matter what season of the year it is (especially in California). But of course, too much sun, too strong and rapid changes of temperature, extreme cold, extreme heat, dense fog, heavy smog, strong winds, etc. should be all avoided. You must use your judgment, and of course, dress the baby appropriately. In many other countries children do get accustomed and enjoy very cold weather. They sleep on terraces under protected roofs while it rains, even snows, outside.

Q. I love to see naked babies in the sun. Is there a danger of too much sun?

A. To expose very young children to direct sun can be dangerous and has to be done with great caution. A baby sleeping outdoors should stay in the shade. An umbrella, a towel can be used to provide shade and adjusted to change as the sunrays move. It is best to expose the legs first and slowly move upward, starting with just one minute. By the time the baby plays in a playpen, which has shade and sun, the baby will move from one area to the other and can be naked! (Sunscreen is recommended). The morning sun is the healthiest — hot, midday sun should be avoided.

Q. Is it all right to leave the baby alone outside?

A. While babies are outside, you should keep checking on them. Ideally, stay at hearing and seeing distance, but still go on and do your own thing. If you start at an early age, your baby will love it and will want to stay outside, will be less inclined to be clingy, naggy, over-dependent, constantly needing company or entertainment. Do not let a baby cry outside. Try and guess what started the crying in the first place. Try to eliminate it, stay out a little with your child and if the crying continues, take the baby inside. But by all means try to take the child out again later. Probably it just was not the right time.

Q. But, what about boredom? Won't the baby get bored outside? How about toys?

A. The stimuli nature provides are unparalleled. Even the youngest infant becomes fascinated by listening to the birds, watching the movements of flies, butterflies, shadows and leaves. Air circulation, temperature change, the playfulness of sunspots and shade are strong stimuli to the skin, the eyes, the lungs, and the metabolism. As the young organism learns to adjust to and cope with constant changes, it becomes more resistant. Of course, the child can also have toys in the playpen or yard. But what a different learning experience your child will have watching nature rather than watching T.V.! I would like to hear from those of you who tried to organize your baby's outdoor life. How did you do it and how did it work out?

**RESPONSI-
BILITY**

In the past the role of being a mother overshadowed the other parts of a woman's personality. As a reaction to old restraints, some mothers want to believe that having a baby should not change their lives. "I live my own life and no child will interfere." Slowly society must realize that parenting is the most important work. Becoming a parent is one of the greatest changes in an adult's life, for better or for worse. Why deny it? Why ignore it? A parent is a parent is a parent, with all the responsibilities, and should be aware of this before he or she becomes a parent. Nobody said it was easy to be a parent. Before becoming one, there are two major difficulties to consider:

1) The On-Goingness of Being a Parent:

You see, even if the child is not home you never stop being a parent. It is a terrific psychological burden knowing and thinking and feeling that "this is my child and I am responsible for his well being." It's kind of a feeling of un-freeness. Think of how you felt before you were a responsible parent.

2) The Technicality of Being a Parent:

This is the nitty-gritty. The basics, if you will. You have just got to do certain things, go through definite care-giving motions while parenting. Whether you want to stay in bed or not, the child still demands on-going care.

It is these two realities that impinge on the attitudes of today. And these realities don't have to be so overwhelming if the parents have strong support, both that of their peers and of society itself. If the parent's job is recognized as tough and society supports parenthood and its toughness, then the parent feels strong. "It is tough, but I'm doing it well" — that's a good way to feel about one of the hardest, most challenging jobs in the world.

I'm not talking about glorifying parenthood the way they did a few years back. They hallelujahed parenthood so much and so greatly out of proportion that no one could live up to that false "perfect" image of the super parent. That was the pitfall of those times. There was lots of support, but it was terribly guilt-inducing.

Cara: Magda, it seems to be so much harder to raise children nowadays. If it weren't for our playgroups and later preschools, most of us parents would be raising our children in a sort of confined and confining monotonous world. We are very isolated from each other. There is no small town, no real community. Our children are as trapped in our adult worlds as we are in theirs. So how can parents give their children any sense of autonomy or self-confidence when they themselves are slaves?

Magda: Parenting takes time. It's like any job you train for. You go to school to learn it, you go through a lot of pressure, exams, sweat, second thoughts, but if you want it badly enough, you keep at it. You can't do your own thing during this job-training period. Society expects you to work hard. After all, it's a job, right? If we could only think of parenthood in these terms. Realistically, parents must know the consequences of their choices — having a child or not having a child, accepting a job or not accepting a job. You see? They must mentally plan for this parenting job as well as physically plan for it. They must make room for this child/job in their lives. If the parents decide that, yes, they choose to have a child, then they must accept the responsibility that goes with that choice. They must accept involvement (time, space, emotion, availability), and a certain giving up of egotistic needs. They must realize this — there is no other way. They must know that there is a certain amount of investment: "I will do this now and later reap the benefits..." And they must really take a good, introspective look at themselves and seriously question: "What kind of person am I?" Then they must also question seriously what a child really needs before they have that child. If parents would think about and plan for parenthood, there would be more happy children, and parents. It's so important for a young child to start with good experiences in his own family. Maybe for two — two and half years, the parents must let go of other activities. Because this kind of timely investment is what ultimately produces secure, independent, self-sufficient children. The more you invest in those first early years of parenting, the easier your life will be later on. You won't have to be a slave to a child who has been given this kind of attention. It's simply the difference between the nagging, neglected (withdrawn or aggressive) children and those that will make it in life independently, with strength and self-confidence.

Cara: Well, what about the single parent or two working parents, who must be away from the child? How can they reap the benefits of that kind of situation?

Magda: If the parents work, and the child is still very important to them, then they must find time for that special quality time. Again, the parents must ask themselves what sort of solution would be satisfying to both them and their child. I believe that if you want something strongly enough, you will find it. I would like to see those parents who can't be with their children find one caregiver with whom they feel confident and comfortable, and pay that person to take care of their children. This helper would feel a commitment and take great interest in the job, since it would involve the most important profession that exists. The parents would feel positive, knowing that they had provided the best, most loving, caring solution. The helper's response to the child's small signals would establish the child's confidence in the adult. This type of confidence forms the basis of contact for the ongoing caregiving.

As an infant advocate over several decades, I've witnessed many changes in attitudes towards infant care in general and group care in particular. Until recently, the care of infants in this country has largely been the concern of the family and the family physician. Only in the last decade or two has the need for providing alternative care become increasingly apparent. In the fifties, group care of infants was non-existent and looked upon as potentially harmful. In the sixties, the pros and cons of group care were debated in an emotionally loaded atmosphere. Since the seventies, an increasing number of infants are spending six, eight, or more hours each weekday in group care.

Though state and federal regulations have been established, even when met, they do not insure that the needs of infants are met, too. In my consulting work with a great variety of centers, I have found that while the people in charge are usually well-meaning, child-loving people wanting to do a decent job, this rarely is possible for the following reasons:

1. Even nationwide, there are very few centers that serve as good models for other infant day care centers.

2. Comprehensive pre-service and ongoing in-service training hardly exist. Having an M.A. in early education does not guarantee enough knowledge in infancy.

3. Both the salary and status of infant care-givers are almost the lowest on the teaching totem pole, resulting in low morale and constantly changing staff.

4. As formal training in infant care is so inadequate and in many places non-existent, centers look for experience. A person may start as an aide in one center, be hired as a teacher later in another, and eventually become a head teacher and director. The problem is that most likely the original experience was gained in a poor setting, which the person then brings to the next center, and thus inadequate centers mush-room.

5. Though many centers have some guidelines, few have developed a working philosophy and a methodology to go with it. Consequently, each care-giver acts according to his/her own beliefs and back-grounds. Infants must continuously adjust to changing people and changing approaches.

6. With very few exceptions, centers weren't built for the purpose of rearing infants. Many times they are quite inadequate; rooms are too large with high ceilings (church rooms), too small without direct exits to safe

DAY CARE CENTERS*

---

*   <u>Education For Parenthood</u>, Conference Report 1981. Co-sponsored by California Task Force on Positive Parenting, Education Development Center, and U.S. Dept. of Education.

outdoor areas, have little or no proper lighting or sun.

7. The requirements of a low adult-infant ratio, which is usually respected, often results in having many big and small bodies in one large room. The noise and activity levels are overwhelming.

8. To keep the cost down whenever possible, volunteers are used. Lately they are recruited from senior citizens chosen for their work availability and other reasons besides their competence to work with infants.

9. Parent training has just begun; therefore few parents know what they should look for or demand of a good infant center.

In spite of much lip service, children, especially infants, are still a low priority in our society. Can any center meet the needs of infants under such difficult conditions?

What are the infant's needs, beyond those for food, rest, warmth, and hygiene? Most people would respond, "love and cognitive stimulation." They try to meet the need for love by rocking, fondling, and body contact. They try to meet the need for cognitive stimulation with objects, teaching materials, and lesson plans. They separate education from routine care-giving activities.

We who follow the RIE philosophy have our own ways of meeting infant needs. We promote the idea of reuniting these two concepts, education and caring. I coined the term "educarer" to emphasize the interdependence between the two concepts.

Our approach is based on the experience of more than three decades of research and clinical work with infants who were reared at the National Methodological Institute of Residential Nurseries in Budapest, Hungary. This institute, commonly called "Loczy," was founded and directed by Dr. Emmi Pikler.

Respect is the guideline of RIE's philosophy. The educarer shows respect by treating the infant as an active participant rather than as a passive recipient in all interactions.

The following outline defines the principles and philosophy we believe in.

1. An infant derives security from a predictable environment, and the opportunity for anticipation and making choices.

2. An infant needs an intimate, stable relationship with one constant person (a mother figure). This relationship can best be developed during individualized care-giving activities.

3. The infant does not need direct teaching or help to achieve natural stages of gross motor and sensory motor development.

4. Infants learn best when allowed to freely move and explore in an environment which is physically safe, cognitively challenging, and emotionally nurturing.

5. The educarer's sensitive observation gives an understanding of the infant's needs.

6. The educarer allows for long uninterrupted times for play and fosters interaction between infants.

RIE seeks to attain a balance between adult stimulation and independent exploration by the infant. We focus on two areas of the infant's life. One is the time spent with the adult who cares for the infant. The other is the time the infant spends alone freely exploring his/her environment. We believe these two areas are interdependent and influence each other. Only a child who receives undivided attention from his/her educarer during all routine care-giving activities will be free and interested to explore his/her environment without needing too much intervention from the educarer. The educarer needs to understand that the infant needs both concentrated attention while being cared for and time to explore alone.

In order to highlight the difference between the attitude of a good average care-giver and a trained educarer, we will give some illustrations to show the two approaches:

- Whereas many care-givers rely on infant curricula, books, and packaged programs as prescriptions to teach, drill, and speed up new skills in the areas of gross motor, social/emotional, or language development, the educarer trusts the infants' abilities to initiate their own activities, choose from available objects, and work on their own projects without interruption;

- Whereas the care-giver teaches and encourages postures and means of locomotion which the infants are not yet able to do on their own, thus hampering free movement and exploration and sometimes even creating bodily discomfort, the educarer provides appropriate space for the infant to freely initiate his/her own movements without interference, thus helping the infant feel comfortable, competent, and self-reliant;

- Whereas the care-giver's attention is focused on the elicited response to his/her stimulation, the educarer focuses upon observing the whole child, his/her reaction to the care-giving person, to the environment, and to peers, thus learning about the child's personality and needs;

- Whereas the care-giver selects and puts objects/toys in the infant's hands, the educarer places the objects/toys so the infant must make an effort to reach and grasp. The child works towards what he/she wants;

- Whereas the care-giver encourages dependency by assuming an active role, such as rescuing a child in distress or helping him/her solve problems, the educarer waits to see if the child is capable of consoling himself/herself and solving his/her own problems, thus encouraging autonomy;

- Whereas the care-giver may often use bottles and/or pacifiers to soothe a crying child, creating a false oral need for food and sucking, the educarer accepts the child's right to show both positive and negative feelings. The educarer does not want to stop the crying, but rather he/she tries to understand and attend to the child's real needs such as sleeplessness, hunger, or cold. If the infant soothes himself/herself by thumb sucking, the educarer accepts this as a positive self-comforting activity;

- Whereas the care-giver often restricts infant-infant interaction, such as infants touching each other, for fear of their hurting each other, the educarer facilitates interactions by closely observing in order to know when to intervene and when not to;

- Whereas, in a situation of conflict between infants, the care-giver resolves the problem by separating, distracting, or deciding who should have the toy or object in question, the educarer would comment, "Both you, John, and you, Anne, want that toy." Often after such impartial comments, minor conflicts resolve themselves;

- Whereas the care-giver may become aggressive in controlling an "aggressor," thereby reinforcing the aggressive behavior, the educarer models appropriate behavior by touching the aggressive child and quietly saying something like, "Easy, gently...nice."

- Whereas the care-giver may rush to pick up, to rescue, and to console the "victim" of the "aggressor," the educarer squats down, touches, and strokes the "victim," saying "Gently, now, nice." By concurrently stroking and talking to both the "victim" and the "aggressor," the educarer is modeling and consoling both children without reinforcing a pattern of becoming a "victim";

- Whereas the care-giver likes to have more people or helpers in the room, the educarer wants to become the steady person to his/her own small group of about four infants;

- Whereas the care-giver gets exhausted from picking up one child and putting down another, as if extinguishing one fire after another, the educarer calmly observes and can often prevent the "fire";

- Whereas the care-giver may swoop up an infant unexpectedly from behind, thereby startling, interrupting, and creating resistance in the infant, the educarer always tells the infant before she/he does any-thing with him or her, thus gets cooperation.

All of these examples try to illustrate that while both the care-giver and the educarer love the infant, the educarer demonstrates love by showing and teaching respect.

The infant educarer has a basic trust in the infant to be an initiator, an explorer, and a self-learner. The role of the educarer is to provide an environment that is physically safe, cognitively challenging, and emotionally nurturing. In addition, the educarer provides time for uninterrupted play and infant-infant interaction. The child is involved actively in all care activities which allow him or her to become a participant rather than a passive recipient. Using sensitive observation, the educarer comes to understand the child's needs.

If educaring appeals to you and you want to apply it in your center, you can get more information from The RIE Manual. You can also check your own attitude to see whether you indeed do follow our philosophy. Ask yourself the following questions:

• Do all infants in your care have enough space available to move in, objects to choose from, time to play without interruption?

• Do you give them your full attention while caring for them?

• Do you wait for them to work out their own conflicts?

• Do you observe closely in order to determine their needs?

• Do you understand behavior from an infant's point of view?

WORKING MOTHERS

Cara: Magda, what about the mother who wants to work?

Magda: If a mother feels more a human being in a "grown-up" world and gets much more self-esteem in that kind of environment, then that happy, fulfilled woman will be a better mother for her child when she comes home. A bitter, frustrated mother at home only makes a child feel guilty. "I sacrificed my life for you..." What a terrible, heavy burden that lays on the child! So, when I say a mother has to work, that can mean for economic or psychological or any other reasons. Quite often when a person says "I <u>have</u> to..." it really means "I <u>want</u> to..." It is not always easy to take a stand and do what you really want to do — and then admit it. I agree that a mother who enjoys her outside job may come home much more refreshed, more ready for being with her child. A parent needs self-time just like a child needs self-time.

And women who choose to be full-time mothers also need time away from their children. Even if it's a single, quiet, private hour a day, a mother must not stifle her individuality for the children. But, I also don't want these same mothers to feel that they <u>must</u> get out, must work, must do something else other than what many of these women really want to do the most; that is staying home and parenting full-time. I still recommend, if it is economically feasible, to wait those first few years before going out into the world on a full-time basis. Sure, it's a sacriface, financially, maybe creatively, but there is time, so much time later. You must ask yourself, "What would really happen if I <u>didn't</u> work right now...?"

Cara: Yes, Magda, think of the mother that must work at an outside job that she doesn't like, then comes home feeling tired and possibly a little defeated, and she must not only find some kind of quality time for her children and her mate (if there is one), but also for <u>herself</u>. No matter what you do and how you do it, the child is still there waiting for some kind of nurturing input. And so is your inner self. The child outside and the one within: they <u>both</u> need attention — recognition — love.

Magda: But, the caring process doesn't have to be an overwhelming one. If the mother provides a rhythmic schedule, a safe environment for the child, then there is a certain degree of predictability and security in that world for both the little one and the mother. So many mothers are still afraid of not being good mothers while they are not with the child. Look, if the mother is in the kitchen three rooms away and the child is in a safe place, then the mother is <u>still</u> the carer. If the child is with another carer, chosen by the mother and also providing this kind of safe, secure environment and rhythmic schedule, then the mother can feel good about that, too. It's a fact that the child needs a mother or a mother figure. And if that child comes home from a day care environment to a mother who shares some total, individual, undivided attention even if for an hour each evening, then that is still mothering. You see, if you give yourself your own space, and your child is in a good place where you really know that the basic needs are met, then you don't have to be so worried, so anxious. If you feel that things are really okay, then you are not worried. You are not only nurturing your own self, but feeling secure in knowing what your child really needs (not gadgets, but respect and individual attention).

Some child care centers are very good, but few are very good for children under two years of age. I am mostly critical of infant day care centers. I still find very few places providing infant care which combine theoretical knowledge with practical skills; the knowing <u>how</u> and the knowing <u>why</u>.

**WISHES
FOR
PARENTS
AND BABIES**

Cara: What kind of wishes do you have for children, for parents?

Magda: First, my wishes for children. I wish they could grow according to their natural pace, sleep when sleepy, eat when hungry, cry when upset, play and explore without being unnecessarily interrupted. To be allowed to grow and blossom as each was meant to be, not molded or shoved into some mode of faddism that confines like a violin case.

I wish children would NOT have to: 1) Perform for their parents; sit up when ready for rolling, walk when ready for crawling. A child can be pushed to do these things, but physiologically may not be really ready. In our culture we push to attain these states faster than they should be reached. 2) I wish children would not have to reassure parents of their effectiveness; i.e. smile when frustrated, clap hands when sleepy — "If my child smiles at me, this shows I am a good parent." 3) Not be ping-pong balls between parents. 4) Not be experimental subjects for toy manufacturers, cereal makers, new fads or theories in child care.

Please parents, the next holiday season, don't succumb to the pressure of buying expensive, complex toys designed to be used certain ways. They rarely give children opportunities to explore and use them in their own way. Toys designed to entertain create passive on-lookers, future T.V. addicts, rather than curious, actively-learning children. Pressures from commercials are especially strong at the holiday time of year. So think. Think of the many children who are lost and bored unless entertained and who keep asking, "What shall I do now?"

And my last wish for children would be that they could communicate to their parents:

> Please let me grow as I be,
> And try to understand why I want to grow like me,
> Not like my mother wants me to be,
> Not like my father hopes I'll be,
> Or like my teacher thinks I should be,
> Please understand and help me grow
> Just like Me!

Cara: And for parents, Magda?

Magda: For parents, I wish a lot of things too. I wish they would: 1) Feel secure, but not rigid. 2) Be accepting, but set limits. 3) Be available, but not intruding. 4) Be patient, but "true to thine ownself." 5) Be realistic, but consistent in their expectations. 6) Have the wisdom to resist new fads. 7) Achieve a balance between giving quality time to their children and to themselves. 8) Achieve a state of self-respect and give equal respect to their children.

And I have a special wish for fathers too. I wish that fathers could assume a new role of fatherhood based on human relationship rather than believing that being warm and gentle is not "manly" or that a father is expected to be tough — to throw the children into the air, or blow cigarette smoke in their faces (yes, I have seen this done "playfully"). Rough-housing not only scares babies, but sometimes causes brain damage. What I'm saying is that playful pummeling is okay as long as it's not forced by the father and hard on the child. I would like fathers to not be afraid to be themselves, to know that just because they are men, being "macho" is not really expected of them. They can be tender and soothing and quiet and still be "manly."

And you know what I wish above all else? That we each don't lose sight of laughter. That through all of the pain we might see and feel around us, we maintain our sense of humor. People who take life too seriously are terrible to live with! Amen!

ON THE IMPOR- TANCE OF DIAPERING

Diapering is a daily responsibility of parents and of professionals caring for infants and toddlers that is usually viewed as an unpleasant chore, a task of hygiene, "time out" from an infant's play and learning. Yet I have many reasons for wanting to write on such a "mundane" subject. Diapering is a universal experience for infants, innumerably repeated during their first two to three years of life. Diapering involves a major component of a young infant's daily care regimen. An average infant in our society is diapered about 5000 times. We are all affected negatively or positively by cumulative experiences in our lives. One of the first cumulative experiences in our lives is diapering, involving much of the child's and parent's time and energy during those first, most impressionable years of the child's life. Yet, is it truly "time-out" from meaningful life for an infant?

Let us take a look at the process of diapering. While being diapered, the baby is close to the carer and can see her face, feel her touch, hear her voice, observe her gestures and learn to anticipate and to know her. A parent who perceives diapering as a chore will often develop a fast, efficient routine, with hygiene as the only goal in mind. Often, toys and rattles are put into the infant's hands to distract the baby's attention from the diapering activity. There is little eye contact or communication, since the parent concentrates on the lower part of the infant's body, sometimes even standing with her back to the baby. And if the infant cries or objects, the parent often hurries even more, consoling the baby, "there, there, in no time we will be through and then we can play together." The outcome of this style of diapering is that it frequently becomes mechanical and depersonalized for efficiency's sake. The infant also receives several negative messages, such as: caring for the body and the body's processes are offensive, and that care activities aren't enjoyable times together. When toys are given to an infant while he is being diapered, the baby is being encouraged to split his attention away from his body, away from the task at hand, and away from relating with his parent.

Yet diapering can be prime time for baby and parent, as enjoyable as playing together, when it is not seen as a chore. Within the process of diapering, there are many opportunities available for the infant in the form of learning experiences, playful interactions and the development of the parents' and infant's relationship. I have designed the following guidelines for making all care activities enjoyable, quality times, rich with invaluable learning experiences.

1) Prepare ahead. Before involving the baby, have everything ready so you won't have to search for a pin, cream, or water, which would disrupt the continuity of your time together.

2) Observe what the child is doing. If he is absorbed, do not interrupt him, but wait for the right moment to intervene.

3) Explain to your child what you are going to do. This pattern can begin in early infancy in all interactions. Although the infant does not understand your words at first, he will soon begin to associate your sounds and tone of voice with your gesture and actions, and his anticipation will grow for enjoyable time shared together with his parents.

4) <u>Communicate with the child</u>. Gently take any toys or objects out of the child's hands, explaining what you are doing, and <u>tell him you want to pick him up now</u>. Reach out and wait for a response. Do not pick up your child unexpectedly or from behind. This pattern is helpful to begin even with very young infants who may not show any visible response at first but it helps foster a style of two-way communication that respectfully involves the child.

5) <u>Explain and show your infant what you are doing, step by step</u>. As you diaper, allow your infant to follow and become involved in the process, to make eye contact, study your face, vocalize, initiate play, follow your actions and respond to you, and you to him.

These guidelines are general, and you will find that, as your infant matures, you will need to continually adapt to your child's age and stage of development. You will need to get a "feel" for your own style of interaction with your particular infant, each of you having distinct personalities. These guidelines are not meant to create another style of "mechanized diapering but to give you and your infant a sense of the importance of his daily care activities and to take fuller advantage of the many opportunities available for the infant through meaningful social and emotional exchange. The social interactions of the infant and parent are full of the unexpected, full of new delights and new challenges.

The framework I have set forth is open enough to allow space within its structure for you to be able to grow with your child, to improvise and respond spontaneously to unexpected behaviors, and to stay cued in and aware of your child as an individual. This "personalized" approach to diapering promotes the development of an infant's positive self-esteem, body awarenes, social attentiveness and responsiveness. It also encourages an infant in the difficult, but crucial and exciting struggle for autonomy. An infant who is encouraged to actively participate in the process of his care will be challenged to be a willingly independent child and to master his own self-care as he grows older. Approaching diapering as quality time with your infant will give you more enjoyable time together, and will give him the feeling that you value your time together, which affirms for your infant his value as a person.

GUIDELINES TO MAKE ALL CARE ACTIVITIES OPTIMAL LEARNING EXPERIENCES

THE DIALOGUE

CARER	INFANT	LEARNING THROUGH:
GREETS CHILD "You seem to be having a good time with your rubber giraffe," TELLS AND SHOWS WHAT SHE IS GOING TO DO. "But I want to pick you up and diaper you."	PAYS ATTENTION	ANTICIPATION ATTENTION AWARENESS
WAITS FOR INFANT'S REACTION. "You're not quite ready so I'll wait a little. (One or two minutes later). Now you seem ready."	RESPONDS TO THE INITIATIONS OF CARER (POSITIVELY OR NEGATIVELY)	RESPONSIVENESS TO EACH OTHER EXPECTATIONS
ASKS FOR COOPERATION OR FOLLOWS CHILD'S LEAD. "First we have to remove your overall. You pull out your foot."	COOPERATES AND PARTICIPATES	THE JOY OF PLEASING AND ACTIVELY PARTICIPATING
ENCOURAGES MASTERY "You helped with this (touches foot), now pull out the other one."	ACHIEVES MASTERY, BECOMES PLAYFUL, TEASING. DOING THE OPPOSITE OF WHAT IS ASKED	MASTERY AUTONOMY
ENTERS THE GAME BUT EVENTUALLY GETS BACK TO (BUSINESS) TASK — (smiling). "This doesn't look like a foot, but more like a hand to me."		SECURITY CHALLENGE
ENJOYS THE PROCESS	ENJOYS THE PROCESS (laughs)	JOY

I feel strongly ambivalent about calling attention to a book that I consider harmful. In our society, a negative response attracts more attention and, therefore, may sell a product better than a positive one. Yet, since several mothers have asked for my opinion on a book with the catchy title "Toilet Training in Less Than A Day" (Simon and Schuster, 1974, N.Y.), I will share my concerns with you.

On the back book cover a photograph shows the smiling authors, Nathan H. Arrin and Richard M. Foxx, squatting, with a child and a musical potty chair between them. The front cover of the book says, "The breakthrough book that describes a professional-tested new method of successful toilet training in one pleasant and exciting learning period." How can even a sensitive, knowledgeable parent resist all that?

The book certainly lays the ground work for credibility. After describing their previous research work with profoundly retarded persons who, with their method could be trained in three days, the authors, both with Ph.D.'s, devised their method for normal children. "Within three or four hours," they write, "the young child had learned to toilet train himself..." (page 10). In case you are not desperate enough about toilet training, here are some of the titles of 23 mother's letters: "Help - 36 months," "At our wits' end - 47 months," "He positively will not - 32 months," "Tried everything - 42 months," "I am desperate - 24 months and 36 months." (pages 13, 14, 18).

The authors then proceed to tell how expensive diapers are, about $200.00 a year for disposables and diaper service, or how much time and energy it costs to do the laundry yourself. But this is minor compared to what you go through with each diapering, which takes "about nine hours per week." (page 21).

In criticizing the "old method" the authors further elaborate on how much of the mother's time that training requires. "She must undress the child, sit him on the chair, remain with him for an extended period, dress him again and empty the potty in which he urinated." (page 24). It sounds like they have difficulties believing that mothers may enjoy being with their children, or lo and behold, even enjoy caring for them.

Obviously one advantage of the "new training method" is speed. Another one, "the pleasantness of the...experience" (page 31) is more questionable. I will sketch some aspects of the procedure so each of you can decide how pleasant, or unpleasant the experience sounds to you for your baby and/or yourself. Throughout the procedure "your intent is to give your child undivided attention and you should not allow any event to interrupt the interaction." (page 47) (no phones, t.v., radio, guests or even family members).

Place: In the kitchen. Aids and Supplies: A potty chair, a doll (which can drink and urinate) for demonstration, many snack items for reward, a variety of drinks for reward, and to fill the child's bladder. "If your child is reluctant to drink..stimulate his thirst by (giving) salty items...by placing the cup against his lips and lifting it..." (page 62). When the child does what the mother wants, reward him with praise, snacks, drinks, hugging, kissing, clapping, "be enthusiastic, exuberant, excited, expressive and let this delight be very visible." (page 70). In addition, you can call on a "supportive crowd of enthusiasts, such as aunt, uncle, friend, Captain Kangaroo, or grandma. Grandma will be so happy."

But what if the child has wet his pants?..."Reprimand him immediately by loudly saying, "No!" "Wetting is bad." "Mommy doesn't like wet pants." (page 84), etc., and then make him practice. "Practice going to the potty chair, practice quickly. Practice pulling your pants down. Practice quickly. Practice getting up quickly, you wet your pants. Practice pulling your pants up, practice quickly." (page 85).

I can not help having a frantic nightmare at this point. I see miniature Charlie Chaplins moving quickly to the potty chair, urinating (potty chair signals), eating salted crackers, drinking more fluid, standing up, pulling pants up, down quickly, quickly faster, faster, stop. It seems like the caricature of a future shock world for children.

The reality is that once a child decides to use the toilet, he knows how to do it. It is unnecessary to teach, practice, exercise the little techniques. Children do learn to dress and undress themselves if parents encourage cooperation every time they care for them. If each diapering has been a pleasurable experience, a true dialogue between parent and child, if the caregiver has given her full attention during all these times, there will be no need for the special circus performance of "The Day" (of the training).

But suggestions to parents to do something unnecessary would not drive me to call a book harmful. In order to convey my concerns I will try to describe how much more is involved in toilet training than just getting urine and feces into the toilet.

Toilet training happens as a result of a healthy, normal child, living in an average accepting, caring family. As part of his natural development the child wants to be like, and act like, his parents. The child has to be ready physically (capacity of the bladder to hold more fluid, better muscle control), cognitively (be fully aware of what he is expected to do), and emotionally (be ready and willing to give up a comfortable situation, such as just letting urine and feces out whenever it does so naturally). For the child it means that he has to delay and control a natural urge, to give away something that he may believe is still part of his body, and therefore valuable, and to conform to an adult-designed and timed routine. It is an area and a time of inner conflict. But like the prince of the fairytale, he, the child, fights his battles and masters the difficulties to gain the love and admiration of his first idol — his parent.

Endless volumes have been written on the consequences of how a child achieves this important milestone on his way to autonomy. In Erik Erikson's famous epigenetic chart(<u>Childhood and Society</u>), the first three critical steps, conflicts or crises a young child must go through are: trust vs. mistrust during infancy, autonomy vs. shame and doubt around toddlerhood, and initiative vs. guilt during the preschool years.

Let us now come back to the book we started with. On page 10 the authors state: "No single theoretical orientation is followed exclusively. The procedure borrows heavily from the many different approaches to children. We have utilized the psychoanalytic emphasis on the possible effect of harsh toilet training on later personality by making the experience a pleasant one." This latter statement shows that the authors have a full misconception of what the psychoanalytic theory is all about. There are few concepts as thoroughly described in psychoanalytic literature as toilet training, the vicissitudes involved, the characteristics of the anal personality, etc. To go into more detail on this huge subject is beyond the scope of this writing. I will mention some of the struggles of early childhood which have an effect throughout our life:

> • dependence or independence and autonomy

> • taking or giving   • holding on or letting go

• progression (wanting to grow up) or regression (wanting to stay a baby)

Though these are lifelong struggles, they seem to be crucial during the anal stage of development. Erikson writes, "This (anal) stage, therefore, becomes decisive for the ratio of love and hate, cooperation and willfulness, freedom of self-expression and its suppression. From a sense of self-control without loss of self-esteem comes a lasting sense of good will and pride; from a sense of loss of self-control and of foreign over-control comes a lasting propensity for doubt and shame." (page 254).

I feel sorry for the parent who tricks and treats his child rather than trusts him. I feel sorry for the child who is manipulated and deprived of making this important step towards autonomy by his own volition.

I believe the "gentle" operant conditioning the book advocates is as harmful and psychologically harsh as any old punitive, bribing, coercing method ever used. It shows no respect or love for the child, but a phony, exuberant, and manipulative joy for his performance. This book is the product of our impatient society looking for instant results, forgetting the importance of every experience in the long process of learning.

SLEEPING*

Dear Magda,

It is becoming more and more difficult to put Alison, my seven-month-old, to sleep. I have always nursed her to sleep, but now she wakes up crying as soon as I put her down, or shortly thereafter I have tried putting her down later and later in the evening, thinking she was not sleepy, but this did not help. Now, neither Alison nor I get enough sleep. Help!

Tired Parent

Dear Parent,

I'll try. But do not expect a magic formula; sometimes we cannot isolate any one problem area from the rest of the everyday life of your baby.

I know that the easiest way to put your baby to sleep is to nurse her to sleep. I have observed, however, that as an infant becomes more aware of herself and of her environment, it is better to put her down while she is still somewhat awake. It is possible that waking up in a crib with no memory of having been put there can be disorienting and scary. Babies younger than Alison may wake up confused because of the sudden change in their sensitive vestibular organization, (i.e. going from a more upright position to lying flat in the crib).

Rather than putting Alison down later and later, I suggest that you sensitively observe the very first signs of tiredness. That is the time a child is ready for sleep. As time goes by, increased tiredness builds resistance — and once the second wind hits, going to sleep becomes an ordeal for both your baby and you. An overtired child sleeps restlessly, wakes up more often during the night and gets up grouchy, way too early in the morning. Stress and overstimulation can also cause exhaustion, irritability and resistance to sleep.

Many parents I have advised have learned with surprise and delight that contrary to their fears, putting babies to bed very early in the evening did not make them wake up earlier in the morning. Indeed, their babies often woke up much later in the morning, adding hours of sleep.

Your goal is to develop good sleeping habits. The easiest way to develop good habits in general is to have a predictable daily life. Young babies thrive on routine. Ideally, daily events of eating, sleeping, bathing, outdoor play, etc. happen around the same time and in the same sequence each day. As the baby is learning to anticipate the next event, many conflicts are eliminated. A mutual adaptation of the biological rhythm of your baby and your family schedule develops. It also enables

---

* Reprinted from Educaring, Volume V, Number 1, Winter 1984.
"Dear Magda/Dear Parent" column.

you, the parent, to plan for those blocks of time when your baby is usually napping or playing peacefully.

But be prepared that there will be times when a child becomes reluctant to fall asleep, e.g. when she comes down with a sickness, shortly before a spurt of new development milestones, or during certain vulnerable times of emotional growth, such as separation anxiety. Your 7-month-old Alison is at a sensitive period for separation anxiety.

Both the amount and the pattern of sleep change from child to child and of course change as a baby grows. Newborn and very young babies alternate periods of sleep with periods of wakefulness six to ten times within 24 hours, with an average of 18 to 21 hours of sleep; two-to-three-year-olds average 12-14 hours of sleep.

Everything that happens to your baby during the day can influence her sleep pattern. Does she spend plenty of time playing outdoors? Building a room-size outdoor playpen is an excellent investment. Napping outdoors is a good habit.

I want to talk a little about how to put a baby to bed. As bedtime approaches, create an atmosphere that becomes progressively slower paced and more quiet. Do you happen to know the lovely book by Margaret Wise Brown, Good Night Moon, in which page by page the room darkens, gradually evoking a sleepy mood? This is the feeling I suggest you work toward.

Repeating a simple pre-bedtime ritual helps your baby to get ready gradually. For example, making a habit of commenting while putting away toys can be helpful: "The ball goes into this basket here in the corner; dolly sits on the top shelf; the toys will stay here until morning when you can play with them again." Such comments build a bridge between 'tonight' and 'tomorrow,' and provide a sense of continuity and security. Then you may continue, "I am going to pull the curtains now, then I will turn off the big light and put on the night light, then I will go into the other room." As Alison grows older, she may take over the role and have such monologues herself.

Some infants have a special bed companion, a 'lovey' such as a Teddy bear or blanket, also referred to as a transitional object. Putting Alison and her lovey to bed, you may talk to the bear, "Have a peaceful rest. I will cover both Alison and you so that the two of you will feel comfortable and cozy. Are you ready for your lullaby?" (You may want to sing or wind up a music box — music is a soothing way to end a day.)

Finally, caress your baby gently and say, "Good night. I'll see you in the morning."

As you see, I am giving you ideas of how you can create an atmosphere conducive to rest. But remember nobody can make another person fall asleep, (short of giving sleeping pills). How to relax and let sleep come is a skill Alison, like everybody else, must learn all by herself. Children also wake up several times during the night and learn how to ease themselves back into sleep (unless they have a need, or get scared).

Your overall attitude can make a difference. Do not feel sorry for "poor baby" who must go to bed — rather remember how good it feels to rest when you are tired, and how nice it feels to wake up refreshed.

INTRODUCTION:

There are no easy steps to anything in this life that is really worthwhile. The following are ten principles which are intended to clarify the foundation of the respectful approach to infant caregiving. "Is respect different from kindness and warmth? The answer is yes. What does it mean to 'respect' infants and toddlers?....The beginning of the answer lies in the ten principles..." (Gonzalez-Mena and Eyer, 1989, p.3)

STEPS:

DO <u>involve</u> the infant in things that concern him and, especially, caregiving chores (such as diapering).

DON'T distract or work around him so you can get the job done faster

I.   remember that babies have long attention spans if they're actually involved in something.

II. consider that you can give the baby a feeling for team work which can become a life-long attitude.

III. realize how much learning goes on in these kinds of interactions.

DO <u>invest</u> in quality time when you are totally available to the infant.

DON'T settle for almost constant time "supervising" without focusing (more than just briefly), when you are only half there.

I.   give the baby privacy - space and time alone.

II. give yourself privacy - space and time alone.

III. think of care activities as quality time, not as chores.

DO <u>respect</u> the baby as an individual, a worthy person.

DON'T treat him as a cute, empty-headed doll to be manipulated.

I.   try to tune in on the baby's real needs — not your own projected needs.

II. really listen to him when he expresses his needs.

III. don't talk about the baby in front of him.

---

* Demonstration Infant Program, directed by Tom Forrest and Magda Gerber.

    IV.   respect the baby's feelings and his right to express them. It's okay to be mad, sad, uncomfortable, etc.

    V.   offer strength to a child in conflict by being available, reflective, neither judgmental or overly sympathetic.

    VI.   help the baby to anticipate what will happen by telling him what you intend to do. Give the baby a chance to respond before you start the action.

DO <u>learn</u> the baby's unique system of communication (cries, sounds, words, movements, gestures, facial expressions, body positions) and teach him yours.

DON'T underestimate his ability to communicate even though his verbal language skills may be non-existent or minimal.

    I.   regard crying as communication and try to understand it, not just respond to it.

    II.   talk to the baby in a natural way using daily language (not baby talk).

    III.   cut down on endless chatter. A small amount of meaningful talk will be listened to.

    IV.   DON'T repeat yourself over and over.

DO <u>be honest</u> about your feelings.

DON'T pretend to feel something you don't or not to feel something you do.

    I.   give appropriate, honest feedback, being careful not to hook the baby on praise.

    II.   try to be aware of sending mixed messages and guard against it.

DO <u>invest</u> in the time and energy to build a total person

DON'T focus just on cognitive development or look at it as separate from total development.

    I.   help the baby learn to use the potential he has, the "whole child."

    II.   help the baby come to see himself as a problem solver.

DO <u>build</u> security by teaching trust.
DON'T teach distrust by being undependable or often inconsistent.

    I.   tell him you are moving or leaving his presence - don't sneak away without telling him.

    II.   be available, if possible, when he really needs you.

    III.   understand he will go through periods when he needs you even more than usual.

DO <u>be concerned</u> about quality of development in each stage.
DON'T worry about reaching development milestones in a hurry.

    I.   don't push the baby to do things he can't do on his own (like sitting up before he's ready). Let him develop on his own at his own pace.

    II.   don't teach the baby — let him learn.

    III.   give the baby plenty of physical freedom.

    IV.   let the baby stimulate himself — respect him for knowing what is best for him.

    V.   try not to promote a "circus atmosphere" where the baby gets conditioned to being entertained.

DO <u>model</u> the behavior you want to teach.
DON'T preach!

    I.   respond to aggression with gentleness if you want to teach gentleness. Don't give aggression for aggression.

    II.   teach sharing by sharing.

    III.   be aware that all you teach is yourself, your attitudes and behaviors.

DO <u>let</u> a baby learn to solve his own problems.
DON'T take away valuable learning opportunities from him.

    I.   try to wait *after* the expression of a need to allow enough time for the child to attempt to satisfy himself.

    II.   when the baby seems "stuck," facilitate the smallest step necessary to enable him to solve the problem himself.

    III.   don't rescue him, constantly make life easier or try to protect him from all problems.

- Heather's daughter but
    remember that ~~babies~~ infants have long
    Attention span if they are actually involved

- don't ~~talk~~ respect the baby
    talk about the baby in front of him

10, not comparing to others

be real

6) example please

Do model aggression - . we put our feelings on the children
    - often they after don't care about it

CONCLUSION:

In order for you, the reader, to become involved, I ask you to summarize for yourself by taking the words underlined and building a single sentence. If you can do it, you got the word of D.I.P. philosophy — maybe even the spirit.*

---

* During her internship with Magda Gerber and Dr. Tom Forrest in the Demonstration Infant Program, in 1976, Janet Gonzalez-Mena, summarized the programs's philosophy in these 10 easy steps. She has since refined the list that serves as the basis for the book Infants, Toddlers, and Caregivers,(Mayfield Publishing Company, Mountain View, California. 1997), which she co-authored with Dianne Widmeyer Eyer.

PART II:

A PHILOSOPHICAL BRIDGE:
FROM HUNGARY TO THE UNITED STATES

MAGDA GERBER
ANN DAVIDSON
PHYLLIS SLETTEN

REFLECTIONS UPON MY WORK WITH DR. PIKLER

Magda Gerber

Who was Dr. Pikler? In many countries she would not need an introduction at all. She, as well as her accomplishments, are well known. She was my children's pediatrician and my professor. Later, I had the privilege of working with her in Budapest, at the National Methodological Institute for Infant Care and Education (which I will refer to as "Loczy," named for the street on which it is located).

I was an average, anxious mother of two daughters, ages six and two, when Dr. Pikler became our pediatrician. What an eye-opening experience that was! So profound and far reaching was Dr. Pikler's influence upon me that I decided to make the study and care of young children my own life's work. To be trained directly by Dr. Pikler cannot be compared with any other kind of training. For years I observed hundreds of infants — in homes, in parks, in institutions. I experienced first hand how to raise a "Pikler baby" from scratch when my son was born.

It was said in Hungary that if you went to the park and observed the children playing there, you could easily tell which ones were the "Pikler babies." They were poised and graceful, alert and friendly and so confidently independent. What, then, is a "Pikler baby"?

The first one was the Piklers' own daughter. The next one hundred grew up in their own homes with their parents instructed by Dr. Pikler as their pediatrician. She visited the newborn baby daily in its home at first, then weekly, spending long hours observing and facilitating the mutual adaptation of the infant and its family. The next "Pikler babies," now numbering over 2,000, spent their first three years at the Loczy Institute. Though raised in a residential setting without their parents, the "Loczy babies" showed the same basic characteristics as the family raised "Pikler babies".

Pikler babies are brought up under special conditions. They each develop without interference at their own rate. No one worries about the date of the "milestones." No one places them in a sitting position before they're ready to sit up alone. No one tries to teach them to stand or walk. No rattles or other objects are put in their hand. Not even a pacifier is put in the mouth. Are they abandoned? Neglected? Ignored? By no means. Their daily lives provide plenty of natural stimulation to keep them interested. Well-selected objects are available to the infants to climb on, to look at, to touch and manipulate; and of course, all the other moving, babbling babies are there to watch and touch and imitate. And naturally, there is space — lots of space in which to move freely and explore. But the infant makes the choices of how to move and what to play with.

At Loczy the babies have freedom to "do their own thing" in a carefully structured environment. Dr. Pikler believed (and it has been reinforced by research) that infants living in an institute derive security from permanency, constancy and anticipation. Time to sleep, time to eat, time to be outside, to explore inside. Within this predictable rhythm of daily life, the infant has time for uninterrupted exploratory play activities, and the careperson has enough time to give individualized, loving attention to each of the Institute's seventy infants during routine care-giving. Even the smallest infant is looked at, handled and talked to as an active, participating individual worthy of respect. This is unhurried quality time.

Why did Dr. Pikler choose this unusual approach while the trend was to stimulate more and teach more? It was the outcome of her studies, observations and experience.

After receiving her medical degree in Vienna while working at the famous Pirquet Clinic, she became particularly interested in the physiology of gross motor development (as it occurs in a healthy, well-cared for infant who is neither restricted nor taught) as contrasted with the usual artificial motor development which is the result of propping, positioning and using restrictive devices (bouncer, infant seat, walkers etc.). Dr. Pikler postulated that not only do these two different practices affect motor development, but they influence all other areas of growth — social — emotional — cognitive and even character formation.

After having successfully raised her own daughter and her private patients by this approach, Dr. Pikler adapted it to the Loczy Institute, founded in 1946, where she was the executive medical director. More than 2,000 infants, many orphaned or with difficult family situations, have been reared at the Institute, and their growth carefully documented and studied to date. The World Health Organization made a grant available in 1969, making possible a longitudinal follow up study of 100 infants raised at Loczy.

Dr. Pikler received many awards and honors, among them was the candidacy for Medical Science in 1968 for her work on the physiology of gross motor development in infancy and early childhood. Yet she was most gratified by letters sent to her from all over the world from "Pikler babies," now grown up, who ask her advice because they want to raise their infants in the same way they were brought up.

Dr. Pikler authored numerous articles and was the consultant on nine films made at Loczy. Her books, translated into several languages, range from popular ones for parents to textbooks for professionals and scientific monographs.

THE LOCZY MODEL OF INFANT CARE

Magda Gerber

Until recently, the care of infants in this country has largely been the concern of the family and the family physician. Only in the last decade or two has the need for providing alternative care become increasingly apparent.

Professional group care of infants, however, is itself in its infancy. Except for a few model programs led by pioneers of group infant care, most centers and day care homes operate with very little preparation or experience. Historically, group care brings to mind the dreary conditions in orphanages where, in spite of proper nutrition and hygiene, mortality was high and most of the children who did survive failed to thrive. In his well-known article on the subject, Spitz (1945) called public attention to the phenomenon that he termed "hospitalism," the devastating effect which institutional care had on infants. The deviant development of these institutionalized children was attributed to lack of sensory stimulation and/or the lack of a close, nurturing relationship.

As a result, most subsequent research on infancy has explored cognitive and/or emotional aspects of development. Emphasis has been placed upon the need for more nurturing-mothering or for more cognitive stimulation, and existing infant programs continue to be influenced by these two approaches. Professionals attempting to meet the infant's need for a nurturing environment might seek to provide a higher adult-child ratio, more body contact between the care-giver and child, and more rocking chairs; those following the cognitive model would buy learning "kits" and develop curriculum aimed at teaching and stimulating the infant.

The purpose of this article is to describe an institution which has a different approach to meeting these important needs of infants: the Emmi Pikler National Methodological Institute for Residential Nurseries, in Budapest, Hungary.[1] The Institute is known as "Loczy," so named for the street upon which it is located. For thirty years, Loczy has been guided by the same unifying philosophy and well-defined methodology, with the daily life of each infant in its care being scientifically observed and studied. Research findings have feedback for continuous improvement of conditions at the Institute.

Dr. Emmi Pikler's Development of Loczy

Loczy is a residence for normal infants from birth to three years of age, with a capacity to serve 70 infants. It was founded in 1946, after World War II had left many infants in Hungary without parents and in need of full-time care. Located in a former private home on a hillside surrounded by large gardens, the Institute has served nearly 2,000 infants who have spent their first three years there. The Institute operates with 70 full-time staff: five medical doctors, six psychologists, 23 carers[2], plus researchers, aides, registered nurses, librarians, administrators, and support staff. Each staff member has a specifically

---

[1] Previously called the National Methodological Institute for Infant Care and Education.
[2] Called "infant-nurse" by the Institute. "Carer" is preferred by the author, rather than caregiver or caretaker, because of the emphasis on caring, not on giving or taking.

defined role to perform in the actual care of the infants or in areas of supervision and research. In addition to their professional education, staff members are trained in the philosophy of Loczy.

The Institute was under continuous direction of its founder, Emmi Pikler, M.D., until her death in 1984. Fully aware of the potential harmful effects of institutional care on infants, Dr. Pikler began Loczy acknowledging that an average family is a far better environment for an infant than even a good institution. Since an institutional setting, by its very nature, is an artificial place in which to raise infants, she exercised great effort to create a meaningful life for the children. Her goal was not only to prevent "hospitalism," but to foster a special relationship with a consistent carer. She was determined to promote genuine involvement in the environment and a growing feeling of individuality in each child.

Dr. Pikler is well-known in Europe for her original ideas on infant rearing. After receiving her medical degree in Vienna, she developed what was to become her life-long interest in the physiology in gross motor development. Her interests focused on the differences in gross motor development of normal children under two different conditions: 1) when motor development is influenced by adult intervention (positioning, exercising, restricting) and 2) when motor development naturally occurs without adult intervention. Dr. Pikler became an advocate of "non-interference" — of letting the infant develop at his own rate. She suggested that by allowing the child freedom of movement, parents would develop respect for their baby's individual tempo and style in other areas of development as well.

Emmi Pikler first applied her hypothesis when raising her own daughter and, as a family pediatrician, she became influential in the way her families raised their infants. Making weekly visits to the homes of these families, she would spend hours observing and facilitating the mutual adaptation of the infant and the family. The children of these first 100 families became the prototypes for the thousands of children who would spend their first years at the Institute. Know as "Loczy Babies", the latter children were described by authorities as "alert", "exploratory", "autonomous" — terms rarely applied to institutionally-raised infants of the 1940's. These initial results prompted greater investigation of conditions at the Institute.

Two respected French authorities on infants, Dr. Myriam David, a child psychiatrist, and Genevieve Appell, psychologist, reported after their first visit to the Institute:

> From the first step into the house one is fascinated by the looks of the children; flourishing babies, with tanned complexions, harmonious proportions and movements, involved for the most part of the day in various activities, in good contact with adults, without being too dependent on them. The groups are peaceful. Among the children

there are astoundingly few conflicts, although interactions begin as early as 4-5 months. (Hermann, 1972, p. 92.).

Intrigued by their first brief visit, Dr. David and Ms. Appell returned to Loczy for an extensive observation. They published their findings in a book, Loczy, ou le Maternage Insolite[3] (1973), which describes the organization and its methodology of infant care.

LOCZY PHILOSOPHY

The following outline gives the essence of the principles and philosophy of Loczy:

I.   An infant living in an institution derives security from a predictable environment and the opportunity for anticipation and making choices.

II. An infant needs an intimate, stable relationship with one constant person (mother figure).

III. This relationship can best be developed during individualized caregiving activities.

IV. Respect is shown by treating the infant as an active participant rather than as a passive recipient in all interactions.

V.   The infant does not need direct teaching or help to achieve natural stages of gross motor and sensorimotor development.

An expansion of these five principles includes the following:

Predictable Environment

The environment that is carefully planned and structured takes into account that infants who are living in their own homes derive security from permanency, constancy, and anticipation (Tardos, 1964). At Loczy, this is done through the careful organization of space, time and interpersonal relations.

---

[3] "Loczy, an Unusual Way of Caring." Translation by Gerber.

Indoor space is at a premium at Loczy. The children of all ages spend the larger part of their days out of doors; each group has its own fully equipped area. There is a wading pool and several large sandboxes with sand piled as high as four to five feet. There are duplicate cribs (both in and out-of-doors) for each child, plus changing tables for each group located on the terraces and in the large gardens. Within a predicatable rhythm of daily life (regular times for sleeping, eating, staying outside and inside, etc.), the infants have time for long periods of uninterrupted exploratory play in a safe environment. The stability of the environment and the time structures of routines provide predictability on a long-range basis.

On an interpersonal level, the infant is encouraged to anticipate what will happen next by telling him about it before it occurs. This provides an opportunity for his active participation and involvement. For example, anticipation within daily routine activities is aided by telling and showing the infant what is going to be done (I'm going to pick you up now...), giving the child time to respond (e.g. reaching out, crying, or showing disinterest), and then respecting the child's reactions whenever possible. The carer differentiates between situations where the child has a real choice (Do you want to be picked up now?) and if the child responds negatively or with disinterest, he is left alone. If no choice is involved the carer does not ask, but states the intended action. (I'm going to pick you up now. It is time to go). The child is picked up.

Mutual understanding, acceptance and respect are promoted when both carer and child learn to anticipate each other's reactions.

Intimate Stable Relationships

The Loczy staff supports the belief that each infant needs to develop an intimate, stable relationship with one constant person. This is one of the most difficult objectives to put into practice in an institutional setting. To achieve this, nine children form a group and they are cared for by the same three carers throughout their entire stay at Loczy, living together as a unit in their own area. Although each carer is fully responsible for the nine infants during her shift, a special attachment is fostered and soon develops between each carer and her "own" three infants in the group. Thus, each carer becomes a mother figure of three children.

By maintaining ongoing records using a Loczy-designed scale and keeping diaries, the carer becomes intimately involved with "her" children, and the children respond by showing a differentiated reaction to their own carers as early as three or four months of age.

Individualized Care Activities

Trust and intimacy between carer and infant can best be developed during routine care-giving activities and these most consistently repeated experiences have a cumulative effect on both infant and carer. If the carer gives total, unhurried attention each time she cares for an infant, he gets "refueled" with human contact and individual attention and is willing to autonomously explore. "As his motility, skills and interest grow, his curiosity and the pleasure in discovery help him to leave the need-fulfilling object...i.e. the carer." (Gerber, 1971, p. 170). These same care activities also offer excellent opportunities for developing cooperation, speech, body image and mutuality in task-oriented experiences. The child is encouraged to be an active participant rather than a passive recipient in these activities.

The interchange between carer and infant during care-giving activities at Loczy is represented by the following schema:

Carer	**Infant**
Obtains attention of infant by greeting him.	Notices carer.
Verbalizes and indicates what is about to happen.	Pays attention to carer.
Waits for infants reaction.	Responds to initiations of carer.
Asks for cooperation, accepts playfulness. Encourages mastery.	Cooperates, participates, teases.[4] Achieves mastery.
Enjoys process.	Enjoys process.

Respect

The guiding spirit in all human interactions is respect. In order to comprehend the application of such an abstract, but often used word, it is helpful to review the behaviors practiced at Loczy which are guided by respect.

- Regardless of age, the infant is never talked about in the third person, but is directly addressed. When adults need to discuss an infant, it is not done in his presence.

- A "dialogue" between carer and infant begins at the earliest age as the carer observes and acknowledges the baby's every response.

- Infants are never forced to do anything. During feedings, for example, the baby is shown the spoon containing food and only when the infant indicates acceptance by opening his mouth is the food put in.

---

[4] Playful teasing (doing the opposite of what is asked or expected) indicates developing trust.

The infant is allowed to anticipate every step of what is about to happen to him. He is never picked up or put down without being told of the impending action. If asked to make a choice between actions, the infant's choice must be respected.

Respect is the guiding principle in situations other than routine care. It can best be defined as selective intervention and is based upon sensitive observation. Knowing when not to interfere is often more important and generally more difficult than indiscriminate intervention.

Whenever possible the carer trusts the infant to solve problems as they occur in his daily existence. When observing a 7-month-old trying to get a ball which is stuck, the carer may just wait or comment, "It's difficult to get that ball out, isn't it?" (Compare this approach with giving the child the ball or physically helping him). In another situation two 14-month-old children are pulling on the same toy. The carer might reflect, "Ann, you want that bear and you, John, want the bear, too." Often the calm tone of the voice of such impartial reflection is enough for the children to solve the conflict in their own way. (Compare this reflective, non-directive attitude with one where the adult becomes the problem solver: "Ann had it first." "If you fight I will take the toy away." "John, take another toy.").

At Loczy, the role of the carer is to facilitate the development of an active child who is challenged by problems, enjoys his autonomy and trusts adults.

No Teaching

Loczy emphasizes that gross-motor and sensory-motor development are best learned while the infant is freely exploring and manipulating in a safe, carefully designed environment. Spontaneous, self-initiated activities by the infant have an essential value for his physical and mental development in that the pleasure evolving from exploration and mastery is self-reinforcing. Subsequently, the infant becomes intrinsically motivated to learn. The Institute ensures this development with the following conditions:

a) Non-restrictive clothing (the children, including the very young babies, are not tucked in or wrapped in blankets, but they are put into large sleeping bags which allow movement),

b) Ample space, which is expanded with the infant's ability to move. When several infants share a common large playpen, an area of 1,550 square inches is alloted each child. The Institute has large room-size playpens, both in and out-of-doors, which allow the children to locomote by rolling, crawling or creeping;

c) Appropriate simple toys. Toys are never put into the infant's hand, but are placed at a reachable distance so that the child has to make an effort to obtain the toy. Once gained, he manipulates the toy as he chooses;

d) To quote Pikler, "The Institute withholds 'teaching' in any form. Under 'teaching' we understand systematic practice of certain motor skills by holding or keeping the child in a certain position, whether by adult or by equipment, or in any way helping him to make movements that he is not yet able to execute by himself in his daily life." (Pikler, 1971, p.57)

The Loczy child is never placed in restrictive equipment such as an infant seat, car seat, swing, bouncer or walker. High chairs are not used, each child is fed on the carer's lap until the child can independently use a chair or bench and table of appropriate size.

Training at Loczy

The care of the infants, training and supervision of staff, and research activities function as an interrelated whole. Because some of the developmental and behavioral goals at Loczy differ from the usual ones, a Developmental Chart (devised by Falk, 1968, 1971) is used for each child. This detailed program chart covers the following major areas of development:

I.   Gross motor activity

II. Manipulation

III. Social relations (in particular, the infant's reactions during routine care-giving activites).

IV. Eating habits

V.   Speech

The purposes of the chart are:

- to keep reliable weekly records

- to provide data for supervision and research

- to evolve a "profile" for each child

- to exert a desirable influence on the carer.

The 100 items which the carer is required to fill out each week for each of her three children are based upon the Loczy principles of infant care. Ideals of cooperation as well as autonomy are built into the scale. The carer refers to a checklist to record the date of emergence of new behaviors as well as their duration. Since the child's reactions are considered to be reflective of each carer's competence, the carer will interact with the child in such a way as to facilitate the desired behavior. For example, in order to facilitate relaxation in a baby of a few weeks' age, the carer will hold him securely, move slowly with him and talk quietly to him. Since the carer must record when the baby is verbalizing, she will respond to his utterances, talk to him and allow enough time for him to respond.

By contrast, gross motor activities are recorded only if they are at the infant's own initiation, with no help or prompting from the carer.

This unique form of charting provides feedback on the quality of care-giving and, as a result, offers positive reinforcement to the attitudes of the carer. In addition, it provides reliable, documentable data for research activities.

Research at Loczy

The fact that Loczy has operated under the same philosophy and methodology for three decades makes it a unique environment for conducting research (Hermann, 1972). Continuous observation and controlled studies have been carried out since 1960 in the areas of gross motor development (Pikler, 1968, 1971, 1972), (Pikler and Tardos, 1969), manipulation (Barkoczi, 1963), (Tardos, 1966), and infant interaction (Vincze, 1970). A longitudinal study funded by the World Health Organization (Falk and Pikler, 1972) documented the continued growth and adjustment to regular family life of "Loczy Babies" following their adoption.

Research is naturalistic at Loczy; infants are observed and their behavior is recorded as they go about their daily routines, rather than under artificial conditions. Investigators are interested in how the infant chooses to utilize his resources, not what he can be made to do. This can best be exemplified by two research studies conducted at the Institute, one study on gross motor skills, the other on infant-infant interaction.

Gross Motor Development

Research on gross motor development has been conducted continuously at Loczy. These studies add another dimension to literature on the same subject. Loczy documents only self-initiated movements of the infant which occur as a result of neurophysiological maturation without any adult interference, help or teaching. Reviewing the literature, Pikler (1971) found no research dealing exclusively with spontaneous occurences of new motor skills. These skills are usually recorded in conjunction with those influenced by adult manipulation, e.g. pulling up, propping, positioning and exercising. Similarly, infant tests (Bayley, Gesell, Illingsworth) that establish norms for the ages when new skills are achieved (sitting, standing, walking) do not clearly define the circumstances under which the child has learned them. This confusion may contribute to the creation of various beliefs, both cross-culturally and within our own culture, about what is necessary or helpful to promote healthy gross motor development.

In an account of 722 children raised at Loczy, the investigators described their movements as well-coordinated, economical and cautious. "The children, without exception, attained the age-appropriate motor skills." (Pikler, 1971, p.

60.) "They (maintain) a stable high activity level during the whole period of learning new motor skills" (Pikler, 1971, p. 70), and "change their postures on average of at least once per minute." (Pikler, 1971, p. 75). This indicates that a child restricted from moving freely is deprived of the long hours of exercising in transitional postures before mastering the next developmental skill.

Infant-Infant Interaction

Except for some early studies by Buhler (1931), Bridges (1933), Freud and Dann (1951), the twin observation of Lichtenberger (1965), and the descriptive observations of Kibbutz-raised infants by Rabin (1955), the potential value of infant-infant interactions has been largely ignored by investigators of infant behavior. Apolloni and Cooke (1975) noted, after reviewing existing literature on the subject, that the interactions between infant and toddler peers familiar with one another has been a little-recognized variable in infant development.

Conditions at Loczy are most favorable to conduct such studies of early peer interactions since the infants grow up in a group and are allowed ample free play and interaction, with little adult intervention. This peer interaction of Loczy children was longitudinally studied over a two-year period by Vincze (1971). The group consisted of nine children, with the greatest age difference being six months. Social interactions were grouped into nine categories:

    I.   Contact by look, smile, sound.

    II.   Initiation of contact by gesture or locomotion.

    III.   Physical contact.

    IV.   Taking away an object.

    V.   Offering or giving something.

    VI.   Imitation/acts performed together.

    VII.   Common activities, acts performed together.

    VIII.   Verbal communication.

    IX.   Simulation of adult attitude towards peers.

In comparing findings on children six to twelve months of age with these of Buhler and others, Vincze noted that although "taking objects from each other occurred quite frequently," the children reflected positive attitudes toward each other:

This age group is not characterized by a large number of conflicts; the social interrelation of the children seems to offer considerable more pleasure than discontent...We were able to record a substantially broader, more lively and colorful range of social contacts than those recorded by Buhler in the experimental situation. Our data seems to be closer to the pattern of social contacts as recorded by Lichtenberger, based on his observations of his own twins. (Vincze, 1971, p. 39.)

Two areas of research have been elaborated upon here. Loczy publishes much of its research work and, in addition publishes textbooks, books for general readership (especially parents), monographs and numerous articles. Loczy has produced eleven educational films on different subjects of infant care and development.

Conclusion and Summary

The theoretical debate concerning whether or not infants should have substitute or supplemental group care available outside of the family setting has abated. The requirements of our society have determined the issue. Now the quest is for improving the quality of infant care (Caldwell, 1974) (Dittman, 1973) (Kagan, 1976) (Provence, 1977) (Ricciuti, 1976). Until recently, infant programs were analogous to infant stimulation programs. The appeal of infant teaching and stimulation appears to be undergoing reconsideration, with concerns about the hazards of overstimulation now being expressed.

We are moving into a period where "the term 'infant stimulation' is misleading and should not be used in identifying educational programs appropriate for young infants and their parents" (Bromwitch, 1977, p. 81). The basic philosophy of Loczy could be represented by Bruner: "There is inherent in the description given of the growth of infant skill and emphasis on self-initiated, intentional behavior. Surely the chief practical recommendation one would have to make...is that the infant should be encouraged to venture, rewarded for venturing his own acts, and sustained against distraction or premature interferences in carrying them out. It is a point of view very alien from such ideas as preventing 'deprivation' or providing enrichment, both of which are highly passive conceptions..." (Bruner, 1973, p. 8).

The Loczy model is proposed as an alternative to what is currently being done in group infant care. Some of its ideals, goals and concepts relative to infant needs and care-giving may differ from those in this country. Acceptance of an ideal or goal does not require obedience to a methodology, however, and it is not suggested that the methods of Loczy should be, or even could be, duplicated in their entirety in the United States. Developed over 30 years in a controlled setting, the Loczy philosophy and principles do have implications for group infant care in this nation and do merit objective study and consideration.

In summary, the Loczy guidelines are:

- **Basic trust in the child as a self-learner and initiator.**

- **An environment for the child that is physically safe, emotionally nurturing and consistent.**

- **Intimate human relation with one primary carer.**

- **Concept-free observation of the child.**

- **Minimal interruption of the child at play, large amounts of time alloted to play.**

- **Independence for the child in movement, choice, activities.**

- **Involvement of the child in all activities with the carer.**

- **Respect for all human beings, including infants.**

Apolloni, T. and P. Cooke, "Peer Behavior Conceptualized Variable Influencing Infant and Toddler Development," <u>American Journal of Orthospsychiatry</u>, Vol. 45, No. 1 (January, 1975).

Bayley, N., <u>Manual for the Bayley Scales of Infant Development</u>, New York: Psychological Corporation, 1969.

Bridges, K., "A Study of Social Development in Early Infancy," <u>Child Development</u>, Vol. 4 (1933): 36-49.

Bromwitch, R.M., "Stimulation in the First Year of Life: A Perspective on Infant Development," <u>Young Children</u>, Vol. 32, No. 2 (1977): 71-82.

Bruner, J.S., "Organization of Early Skilled Action," <u>Child Development</u>, Vol. 44 (1973): 1-111.

Buhler, "The Social Behavior of Children," <u>Handbook of Child Psychology</u>, edited by C. Muchison. Worcesterter, Mass; Clark University Press, 1931.

Caldwell, B., "Can Young Children Have a Quality Life in Day Care?" <u>Providing the Best for Young Children</u>, edited by J. McCarthy and C.R. May. Washington, D.C.: National Associaton for Education of Young Children, 1974.

Dittman, L., <u>The Infants We Care For</u>, Washington, D.C.; National Association for Education of Young Children, 1973.

Freud, A. and S. Dann, "An Experiment in Group Upbringing," <u>Psychoanalytic Study of the Child</u>, New York: International Universities Press, Vol. 5 (1951): 127-168.

Gerber, M., "Infants' Expression — The Art of Becoming," <u>Psychiatry and Art</u>, edited by I. Jakab Karzer. Basel, Switerland and New York, Vol. 3 (1971): 170-175.

Gesell, A. and C. Amatruda, <u>Developmental Diagnosis</u>, New York: Harper and Kew, Inc., 1964.

Hermann A. and S. Komlosi, <u>Early Child Care in Hungary</u>, International Monography Series on Early Child Care. London: Gordon and Breach (1972): 92-95, 111.

Illingworth, R.S., <u>An Introduction to Developmental Assessment in the First Year</u>, London: National Spastic Society, 1962.

Kagan, J., "The Effect of Day Care on the Infant," manuscript. Cambridge, Mass.: Harvard University, 1976.

Pikler, E., "Learning of Motor Skills on the Basis of Self-Induced Movements," Exceptional Infant: Studies in Abnormalitites, Vol. 2 New York; Brunner Mazel, 1971.

Pikler, E., "Some Contributions to the Study of the Gross Motor Development of Children," Journal of Genetic Psychology, Vol. 113 (1968): 27-39.

Pikler, E., "Data on Gross Motor Development of the Infant," Early Child Development and Care, Vol. 1 (1972): 297-310.

Provence, S., et. al. "The Day-to-Day Experience for Infants and Toddlers," The Challenge of Day Care, New Haven, Yale University Press: (1977) 90-144.

Rabin, M., Growing Up in the Kibbutz, New York: Suringer Press, 1965.

Ricciuti, H.N., "Effects of Infant Day Care Experience on Behavior and Development: Research and Implications for Social Policy," Manuscript. Ithaca, N.Y.: Cornell University (October, 1976).

Spitz, R.A., "Hospitalism: An Inquiry into the Genesis of Psychiatric Conditions in Early Childhood," Psychoanalytic Study of the Child, Vol. 1 New York: International Universities Press (1945): 53-74.

Vincze, Maria, M.D., "Examination on the Social Contacts of Infants and Young Children Reared Together." Magyar Pszichologiai Szemle. Budapest, Hungary (1971).

HAVE
INFANTS
BEEN
CARED FOR
WITH
RESPECT?

Magda Gerber
December 1975

This article is included in <u>Supporting the Growth of Infants, Toddlers and Parents</u>, E. Jones, editor, published in 1979 by Pacific Oaks College, Pasadena, California.

Is infancy a virgin island or an over-invaded territory? Both. We all have been there, yet no one remembers it. We try to study it but what we see reflects the view in the eye of the beholder.

The investigator who studies this "forgotten county" does not speak or understand the language or customs of the "natives"; he is informed by other "interpreters," the adults. What the investigator chooses to study, what he will see and understand, how he will interpret it will be influenced by his background (e.g. ethological, psychoanalytical, developmental or learning theory), or his profession (parent, clinician, researcher, caregiver, etc.).

The infant has endured being regarded and treated as a miniature adult, an empty vessel, a bundle of confusion, a responsive organism, ignorant, competent, the helplessly manipulated and the active manipulator.

His needs have been interpreted and explained. He needs to be:

- tightly swaddled to prevent him from moving

- kept naked to have skin contact

- tied to a board to be straightened

- carried on the mother's body to thrive on her heartbeat

- propped in an infant seat to see more

- put in a walker to move more

- left in a crib not to be spoiled

- stimulated from birth not to get bored

Parents were told to breastfeed, bottle feed, wean abruptly, wean gradually, start solids at birth, breastfeed for years, feed according to the clock, feed according to demand, to give a pacifier, to pull out the thumb, to allow the thumb, not to give the pacifier, both...neither. To sleep with the infant in their bed, to let him sleep alone in his room, to toilet train in less than a day, to just wait and not train at all, to teach their baby and accelerate his learning, to let him unfold at his own pace, to stimulate him in day care centers, or nurture him at home.

And the infant? What does he say? He adjusts or he revolts. When he adjusts and keeps quiet it is taken as proof that what we did was good for him. And when he cries the circle begins. We put him down or pick him up: we rock him or ignore him, feed him, play with him, put him in a bouncer, give him a new toy. One sometimes wonders — the infant must be miraculously resilient, or is he? If we look around the adult population, we wonder if perhaps we pay a high price for adapting to such a confused up-bringing.

We are becoming more and more aware of the importance of the first three years of life as a crucial time when basic patterns of coping, living and learning are set. This is evidenced by the recent abundance of publications on infancy. Yet they bring about more controversy among professionals, and parents are caught in the middle again.

Some believe "parenting" should be taught to those in their teens or even earlier. Some see the need to provide quality alternative infant care services such as day care centers, drop-in centers, family day care homes, etc. In spite of the growing numbers of pamphlets and curricula for group care, there are too few places with a basic philosophy where training, planning and its implementation are integrated into a consistent program.

The Emmi Pikler National Methodological Institute for Residential Nurseries[1], is a residence for normal infants from birth to three years of age in need of full-time care in Budapest, Hungary. From its founding in 1946 until her death in 1984, it was under the direction of Emmi Pikler, M.D. When Loczy was founded I worked with Dr. Pikler in training infant-care nurses.

Upon my arrival in the United States in 1957, I looked for opportunities to continue my work with infants. But not until the mid-sixties did some interest emerge in infancy, parenting, and alternative group care. Finally in 1968 I organized a pilot program for infants and their parents (Gerber, 1971). Since 1972 I have been co-director with Thomas Forrest, M.D., pediatric neurologist, of the Demonstration Infant Program (DIP) at the Children's Health Council in Palo Alto, California[2].

Though our program deserves a more thorough presentation, the following is a brief introduction. We are a preventive mental health program, not a day care center. As its title indicates, our program is based on <u>demonstration</u>. We designed an infant-oriented environment that encourages the infant to become an attentive, actively-exploring person who is self-rewarded in his mastery of new tasks. The infant is given space to move in, appropriate objects to manipulate and other babies to watch and imitate.

---

[1] Formerly known as the National Methodological Institute for Residential Nurseries.

[2] Since the time this article was written I have discontinued my work with D.I.P. and am now full-time director of Resources for Infant Educarers in Los Angeles, California.

We have no more than 4-5 infants of similar ages in one group with meetings once a week for two hours. The ages of our infants in all groups range from 5 to 24 months. Normal and atypical infants are integrated and thus given the opportunity to interact in these small groups. One staff member is in charge in the play room for the 4-5 infants, while the other staff member observes the session and discusses it with the mothers, visitors and trainees in the observation room.

During the infant sessions, either Dr. Forrest, myself, or a trainee is in with the infants and demonstrates special methods of selective intervention (the emphasis being on when <u>not</u> to intervene) that allows the child to reveal himself, to make his own choices and to evolve his own style of mastery. Everyday problems are the curriculum. Dealing with separation anxiety, handling aggression and reinforcing rules are some of the major areas of parental concern and we model how these can be dealt with as they evolve. In every situation we give the child time and opportunity to solve his problems in his own way.

We also conduct an intensive four and half month training program twice a year for 5 to 6 professionals from varying backgrounds who plan to work with infants and parents or train infant carers themselves. These trainees observe, discuss, attend lectures, write reports, make home visits, go on field trips and eventually become "demonstators."

DIP also provides ongoing consultation services to day care centers. We visit and evaluate the centers with our trainees, organize workshops for the centers' personnel and invite them to observe our demonstation sessions.

Infant and parent education as well as training and consulation occur simultaneously. They are interwoven, creating the matrix of DIP. It is one thing to present a philosophy of child rearing, but no matter how impressive it may sound, it is quite another to apply it in everyday situations. This is why our program is based on demonstation. Though directly we only reach small numbers of infants and mothers and trainees, we are a visible model which shows how respect is our guideline everytime an adult talks to, cares for and even thinks of infants.

In the past, the care of the infants was the private business of each family. In spite of all the heated debates as to pros and cons, day care centers for infants are now a reality — for better or worse. These centers are supported by public funds — your money, my money. We are, and should be, concerned that the care we provide leaves our infants unharmed, self-reliant and authentic.

**A CONVERSA-
TION WITH
INFANT
SPECIALIST,
MAGDA
GERBER**

**...ABOUT THE
DEMONSTRA-
TION INFANT
PROGRAM**

Excerpted from
the Children's
Health Council
(CHC) Newsletter

One of the most intriguing and exciting new programs at CHC is the Demonstration Infant Program (DIP). "Commentary" had an opportunity to interview infant specialist Magda Gerber, who commutes from Los Angeles to conduct this program with CHC staff member Dr. Tom Forrest.

Q. Mrs. Gerber, what needs does this infant program fulfill?

A. Today's mothers of babies are in greater need of guidance than ever before. They live under greater pressure, they have less help, and they are flooded with contradictory advice. Bringing up a "normal" child can be a difficult task for an inexperienced mother. If the child has any handicap, this task becomes more complex and may lead to a distressed child/perplexed mother syndrome. I put "normal" into quotes to express the vagueness of the definition. In my work with infants and their mothers, I do not like to use labels. Instead, I prefer to discuss the individual strengths and weaknesses of both the infant and the parent.

Q. Isn't what you are doing educating the parents?

A. Sure, but isn't preparation for all trades and professions necessary? We train plumbers, teachers, engineers — but we provide nothing for those who will become parents, the most important profession. Parents have tremendous responsiblity — they guide our future generations. If you can help parents to perceive and accept the child at his own developmental level, and to learn how to understand and respond to his needs, you can prevent problems before they develop, rather than having the difficult job of undoing them later in life. In our program, parents are guided to learn how to observe, understand, respect and enjoy the individuality of their own and other infants.

Q. Can you give us an example of how this program works?

A. Six-month old Beverly* is a good example of the value of prevention. Beverly was brought to Dr. Tom Forrest, pediatric neurologist and director of the DIP, for diagnostic evaluation. The problem? Beverly had been crying almost constantly since birth. The parents were becoming more and more irritable, feeling helpless, frustrated, angry and guilty. These feelings permeated their lives, their marriage and, of course, their whole relationship with the baby.

---

* Not her real name.

Q. What was wrong with Beverly?

A. Dr. Forrest's examination showed no evidence of neurological deficit. Beverly, a big, strong, healthy-looking six-month old, was "walked" in by her parents, held in an upright position, her body as stiff as a wooden board. While this might have looked like an advanced position for her age, she was completely immobilized, and when placed on the floor, maintained a stiff posture and did not move. Beverly joined a group of three babies ranging in age from seven to twelve months. Her mother was surprised to see them peacefully exploring their environment, and even more surprised to see their mothers say good-bye to the babies and withdraw into the adjacent observation room. The first hour Beverly spent with us in DIP she screamed for the entire hour, seemingly nearly bursting with anger.

Q. How was the program able to help Beverly, or the other children?

A. In our infant-oriented environment, which encourages the infant to become an attentive, active, exploring person, Beverly and the other babies are learning to become interested and self-rewarded in their mastery of new tasks. The babies are given space, equipment to move in, appropriate objects to manipulate and other babies to watch and imitate.

Q. Do infants so young actually learn from each other?

A. Yes, although it is not widely known, we have observed that infants do a great deal of learning from each other, even at a very early age.

Q. How do the parents learn from this program?

A. Dr. Forrest sits in the observation room with the mothers and/or fathers and explains to them while I demonstrate with the infants when to intervene in an infant's activity and when to let him alone so that he learns how to solve his own problems.

Q. Have you had much success with the projects?

A. Let's take Beverly, for example. By now, her sixth visit to the DIP, instead of crying constantly, she interacts with other babies, plays with toys, moves about the room and only cries momentarily. It is quite possible that, had Beverly not come to the DIP, she would have further developed a vicious circle of incomplete problem solving, becoming frustrated and angry, immobilized by her angry crying, so that all attempts to help would become futile, producing frustation and anger in those around her, etc., etc. And this can happen to a healthy, normal, bright child and to well-meaning, good parents.

✳✳✳

Working with children with various disabilities, the Children's Health Council has recognized the crucial importance of the first years of life, and with a grant from the Hancock Foundation, had made this Infant Project possible. The main goal in working with infants at this early age is to <u>detect</u> problem areas, to <u>correct</u> them before they become a part of the personality, and thus to prevent later difficulties. Enrollment in the project was open to normal, high-risk and distressed infants from birth to 18 months.

This was a particularly rich session because Magda was being interviewed by a Palo Alto Times reporter for an article on the program.

In answering the question as to why the program exists, Magda remarked that parents these days hear many theories about how to develop independence in children and they feel they need help in sorting out the workable ideas. Many parents feel weary from the relentless ongoing life with a dependent child. Parents have needs too, which often get shortcut when faced with a nagging child. There is an easier way of life with a child which is demonstrated in the process of the class.

It is easiest to begin at the beginning, and the earlier one develops a mutually-fulfilling relationship with the child, the easier one's future is likely to be. The problem is that the newborn is so cuddly, and that the culture tells the mother not to leave the child alone. The result is that too often the mother thinks she should give everything to the child: stimulation, teaching, and cuddling. She tends to build up expectations for herself which are impossible to fulfill, as well as developing expectations in the child which she will later be unable to meet.

The Demonstration Program believes that the child should be allowed to do what he wants. The adult should intervene only for selected reasons. Most adults are always telling a child what to do and what not to do. What they should be doing is reflecting the child's experience — entering the child's world rather than imposing their own ideas on him. The adult should be observing how the child solves his problems. Take, for example, the problem of two children tugging on the same toy. If the children are about the same age (and children don't need to play with others from another age group) the adult can take a non-interfering role. Rather than interfere, _reflect_. Just say, "Daniel wants the toy. Daryl wants the toy." Be a sports announcer. "So-and-so has the ball." "Now Daniel cries for the ball." This monologue is all based on the assumption that the child is getting the message that "I am with you. I don't abandon you." What the adult is not doing here is deciding Daryl had the toy first and should therefore keep it. The child has the opportunity to learn the process of working it out. The adult stays calm. The adult doesn't take over the problem-solving for the child.

Magda prefers simple toys for children, toys that represent one principle or process, and toys that children can manipulate and "work" for themselves. Something not in this category is a music box that the adult has to wind up for the child. A goal of children's play is that the child learns what he can do. The adult should not be feeding him preconceived ideas about how it "works".

A child has a long attention span when allowed to do his own inner task, but he can be easily distracted. Part of the goal of DIP is to allow concentration. The children in the program are at ease together or alone. They are free in their going outdoors and coming in. The ideal is one adult in the room with a small

NOTES ON THE DEM- ONSTRATION INFANT PROGRAM:

One Session, September 25, 1974

Notes by Phyllis Sletten (a participating mother)

group of children (five children per adult is the maximum for a workable group). This reflects the idea that the family is the best place for the child. His movement out into the world should be a gradual one, but in our culture he jumps from family to school, or from family to a child care center where a large group of children (130) is supervised by too few adults (5). This is too confusing for the child, too noisy. There is a very little focusing, very little attention to each child's needs. Here at the Program there is a soft atmosphere - each child is free to become himself. With no more than 5 children for the adult to watch, there are few, if any, minor accidents. It is necessary to watch children carefully, but the atmosphere should be relaxed. Then the children will take over. If there is an accident or a hurt, they will seek out the adult. If a child falls and cries, try to moderate your own anxiety and don't rescue the child. Often it is the adult's reaction which frightens the child into feeling hurt.

The table and stools in the Demonstration Room (like all the equipment) promote independence. A child can sit anywhere on a stool and it "works" — unlike a chair. One shouldn't grab a child to eat, but allow him to come up to the table and to walk away when he is finished. He can sit at the table and eat or move away and play. The child makes choices, but with clear cut results. If he chooses to play, he cannot take his food with him. If he prefers to eat, he must sit at the table. This process teaches making choices, autonomy and self-reliance. Magda doesn't like highchairs. She doesn't like to imprison the child — it makes him a victim. If he really wants to eat, he will stay at the table. The food needn't be kept out for a long time. It should be put away after meal time. This also teaches the child something. It is not necessary to punish, but it is necessary to teach consequences. The child learns that food is available for a time and then is unavailable. After many repetitions, the child learns.

Children will often reflect the inner mood of the caretaker, i.e. uncertainty, phoniness vs. resolution, honesty. If the caretaker doesn't want certain behaviors she should say, "I don't want you to do that. You want to take the cracker away from the table. I don't want that." Her tone and manner should clearly state, "I am the boss." The adult shouldn't interfere with the child's play. The child can play with anything as long as he wants. ("Anything" here meaning toy or allowed object). But the caretaker is in definite control of some things. Some parents don't allow the child to play freely but do allow the child to spill crackers all over the house, the parent seething inside because of the mess, but too exhausted to enforce another "direction." Parents should be open about their own idiosyncracies. They should make it clear to the child that they are annoyed by too much noise, mess, whatever. What harms a child is for the parent to be intoning "sweetheart" while boiling inside.

Children observe others and imitate — a two-way process.

On the subject of "separation," mothers have the same anxiety as children. Magda likes the child to be <u>active</u> in the process of separation. This is the key to working it out. We should not have active adults manipulating children. In the Demonstration Room mothers come in and sit down with their child. Eventually the child ventures away. The conflict in this process is visible. The child will look away and come back (to mother). Abraham Maslow in Toward a Psychology of Being describes this process of holding on and letting go, which continues one's whole life long. We can see these conflicting needs at play in the adult's attitude toward ideas and possessions. Maslow says we live between now holding on and now letting go. This is a life-long struggle. We hold on when we feel insecure and go out to venture when we feel good. In order to promote "letting go," the caretaker should make venturing more desirable. The Demonstration Program provides a model for the separation process. The room is attractive and the other children also provide interest. The child is allowed to leave his mother. He can check back if he needs to. When the mother leaves is up to her. If the mother is needed later, the caretaker can call her. The child may cry when the mother leaves. Magda believes the child has the right to cry. The caretaker should not tell the child not to cry. One should pay attention to the child, acknowledge that he is sad. We can't protect the child from all events which will upset him. Some mothers become very anxious when their child is crying. It is helpful to separate the disturbance one feels for oneself from the wish that the child would stop crying for his own sake. The Program tries to let the child anticipate what will happen. For instance, before the mothers come back they are "announced." "Now Andy's mother will come in." The child's anticipation allows him to participate in what's happening. Magda feels it is important to say "goodbye" before leaving a child. We are trying to teach children to make choices and take consequences so the mothers must do the same.

When a child falls, he shouldn't be "rescued." A child really gets scared if the parent makes a big deal out of a fall. If the child is really scared, and the parent says "Don't cry," or "Poor baby, let me give it a kiss," (implying "as long as you have me you don't have to worry"), the adult's feelings are being expressed. What is preferable for the development of an authentic child is for the parent to enter the child's experience. Sitting down right beside the child, he is given full attention and empathy. The parent gets close but doesn't pick up the child. The child is allowed to choose if he wants to be held. This reaction on the part of the parent helps the child to be more authentic.

In a situation where two children are fighting, the caretaker should reflect the situation. This will have a calming effect. There should be no favoring of one child over the other. If one becomes the victim and one the aggressor and the situation is not too serious, it is best to let them alone. If one child is hitting, kicking, or biting, most people would become aggressive with the aggressor. Magda prefers becoming gentle with the aggressor. Stoke him gently while saying, "Easy, gentle," with a very calm voice. Do not rescue the victim. Show understanding and be available. We don't want to make being the victim too desirable. It's best to keep a non-judgmental attitude. "That's how things go."

Children in the Demonstration Room are not allowed to climb on the table. In order to teach this the caretaker must keep reinforcing the rule. She says,

"I do not want you to climb on this table," forcibly, and if the child doesn't respond, he is physically removed from the table.

Magda believes that the child should be treated with <u>respect</u> right from the beginning of life. Often children are manipulated like objects. An example of this would be picking a child up abruptly from behind or placing mobiles to be directly over the child on the changing table so he is always distracted from what is happening to him. One should never pick up a child without telling him what your are going to do. Tell him with <u>basic honesty</u>. Don't say, "Do you want me to pick you up?", when it is not his choice at all. Parents can start a dialogue with their child even from birth. In talking with a child, it is important to <u>reflect</u> his feelings rather than subject him to constant flow of "do's and don'ts." It is also important to help a child <u>anticipate</u>. Children need real togetherness. The quality of caregiving is what is important. Baby and mother and father need time alone. All these things enhance the development of a child who is more secure and less dependent.

Listed below are some common-sense practical suggestions for how to enhance the time you spend talking with your child. Many of these you probably do naturally already. Being aware of them, however, may help to make your verbal interactions with your child more meaningful and more helpful to him.

I. **Comprehensive**

Children comprehend language before they produce it. They need to hear language before they can learn it. Without, "doing anything" your child will learn. However, you can enhance and faciliate language development by:

A. Self-talk

Describe on-going actions, events and activities in short, simple sentences. Stick to the here-and-now. Comment informally on what you're doing as you're doing it.

eg. I'm peeling the carrot.

I'm fixing the sink.

Daddy's tired — Daddy's resting.

This is Mommy's sock.

I'm washing your neck.

B. Announce what's going to happen, describe what is happening and comment on what just happened.

eg. I'm going to put on your shoe.

I'm going to open the can.

Mary wants juice, too.

The dog is running away.

The doorbell rang.

The baby fell down.

The juice spilled.

C. Parallel-talk

Comment on what the child (or others) is doing. Describe what he/she may be doing, seeing, hearing or feeling.

eg. You hear the telephone ringing.

That feels cold.

You're climbing high.

You're running down fast.

You want to go on the slide, too.

It's hard to wait.

You don't like being wet.

II. Production

A. <u>Be responsive</u>

Be responsive to your child's speech and vocalizations. Acknowledge him/her when he/she does speak. If his remarks go unnoticed, he'll be less likely to want to talk in the future. Make talking pay off. Give words and vocalizations power. Acknowledge any intelligible words or phrases with recognition.

eg.   Yes — you see a bus. A big bus.

Yes — that's your spoon.

Oh — you want more crackers.

B. <u>Encourage the use of words your child knows</u>.

eg.   Offer a choice involving a single word or short-phrase answer.

Do you want the cookie or the apple?

Do you want the car or the truck?

C. <u>Encourage, but don't demand, imitation</u>.

When you use short phrases that the child can handle, he is more likely to try to imitate key words. Later, after practice, he will be able to produce them on his own.

D. <u>Supply missing, needed words</u>.

If your child becomes frustrated over not being able to express himself, give him a key word or short phrase which he may learn to use in future situations. If he vocalizes and you can guess the meaning from the context, supply the word (words) in a short phrase, perhaps repeating it twice for emphasis.

eg.   Oh — you want a turn.

Say — "my turn."

You want a cookie too — cookie.

E. <u>Expand your child's utterance</u>.

If your child attempts a word, repeat it for him to hear again. Gradually his approximations will come closer to the adult model. If he uses one word, you might expand his utterance to a short phrase while acknowledging it. If he uses 2-3 word combinations, expand that utterance filling in some words he may have left out or adding some new information.

eg.	child: ba	adult:	<u>ball</u>, there's your ball.
	child: bus	adult:	yes, that's a bus.
	child: ride bike	adult:	Right, the man is riding that bike.
	child: Mommy car	adult:	Yes, that's Mommy's car.
		or	Mommy is in the car.
		or	Mommy went away in the car.

F. Ask questions that your child can answer. Ask questions that present choices.

eg. Do you want the car or the ball?

Do you want the big car or the little car?

＊＊＊

Ann Davidson is an author and poet who, as a speech pathologist and language therapist, worked with speech-impaired young children at the Children's Health Council, Palo Alto, California. She was a consultant to the Demonstration Infant Program and incorporated the D.I.P. philosophy into her suggestions.

WHAT IS APPROPRIATE "CURRICULUM" FOR INFANTS AND TODDLERS ?

Magda Gerber

In the last decade a growing number of infant programs have been established in the United States. Some are designed to provide alternative-care environments to the home, while others, referred to as early intervention programs, are geared to stimulate and educate the handicapped, the retarded, or otherwise disadvantaged infants.

Preceding the development of these centers, any number of scientific publications including books, articles, and journals for professionals and the public at large, have popularized new research findings on infancy. Most reports have emphasized that infants are capable of a wider range of activities and learning than was previously believed. In one single volume, entitled The Competent Infant, more than two hundred studies are published in an abbreviated form dealing only with the first 15 months of infancy. (Stone, Smith, Murphy, 1973).

These studies convinced many that if infants can learn, we must teach them. Thus, many current projects emphasize "cognitive development" and are often specific-achievement-oriented. Their curricula are based on levels of performance as defined by various infant studies and tests (Bayley, 1969, Gesell, 1940, Piaget, 1963) and their goals are to enhance achievement. Specific methods are also designed to teach, drill and exercise certain milestones. In addition, there are home-teaching programs which are intended to educate mothers and families in areas of infant stimulation (Gordon, 1970, Painter, 1971). Generally the program staff have preconceived ideas as to when, how, why, and for how long infants should be stimulated. Many times, the principle of "the more the better" is carried out. It is assumed that while all infants would benefit from early sensory stimulation, it is a "must" for handicapped infants to prevent or ameliorate retardation.

A large number of books, packages, programs and infant curricula are available and used as prescriptions in many infant programs. They often serve as guidelines or crutches to carers who may be inadequately prepared in the field of infancy or the needs of the "special" child.

I am proposing a different theory on how infants learn and on how we can facilitate that learning. In the past ten years I have initiated and directed two infant programs based on a humanistic-therapeutic approach to young children. Both were preventive mental health programs, designed to demonstrate infant care for "normal", as well as "high risk"[1] infants. These programs were based on my own experience and background as an infant specialist and child therapist. The overall therapeutic goal was two-fold: 1) to help parents to develop, from the beginning, sound patterns of living with their babies, whether "normal" or handi-capped," and

---

[1] Some early high risk signs: hypo or hypertonia, limpness, rigidity, high-pitched or poor cry, absence of progressive orientation to light and sound, apathy, restlessness, irritability, hyperkineses, lack of eye contact, body resistance to physical contact with mother, lack of response to stimuli, feeding problems, sleeping problems or impaired developmental level with no apparent physical cause.

2) to train "infant carers"[2], professionals who provide group care for infants in different environments (e.g. centers, or family homes). (Gerber, 1971).

Our programs in Los Angeles[3] and Palo Alto[4], California varied considerably from the types of programs described earlier. Our approach was essentially based on the experience of more than a quarter-century of research and clinical work with infants who were reared at the National Methodological Institute of Residental Nurseries in Budapest, Hungary (popularly called "Loczy"[5]).

The following outline defines the principles and philosophy of Loczy.

1. An infant living in an institution derives security from a <u>predictable environment</u>, and the opportunity for <u>anticipation</u> and <u>making choices</u>.

2. An infant needs an <u>intimate, stable relationship</u> with one constant person (a mother figure). This relationship can best be developed during <u>individualized care-giving activities</u>.

3. <u>Respect</u> is shown by treating the infant as an active participant, rather than as a passive recipient in all interaction.

4. The infant <u>does not need direct teaching or help</u> to achieve natural stages of gross motor and sensory-motor development. (Pikler, 1971).

The approach to infants at Loczy is based on achieving a balance between adult stimulation and independent exploration by the infant. Infants are exposed to adult stimulation by the infant carers during all care-giving activities (e.g. feeding, bathing, dressing, etc.). These are unhurried, pleasurable times for both adults and infants. Because these activities occur during the necessary daily routines of infant care, stimulation is constant and consistent. In contrast, in the areas of gross-motor development and fine-motor manipulation, the staff of Loczy does not interfere or promote, but rather relies on maturation and development at the infant's own pace.[6]

In our California programs, the emphasis is similarly on observation, anticipation and selective intervention. Observing her child helps the mother or carer to learn about individual characterestics of her child and to realize what she can reasonably expect of him[7] at any given developmental level. This, in turn, helps the mother synchronize her behavior with the child's needs, tempo and style. Antici-

---

2   "Carer" is preferred by the author, to care-giver or care-taker because of the emphasis on caring, rather than on giving or taking. It will be used for the caring person, whether parent of professional.

3   Pilot Infant Program, Dubnoff Center, North Hollywood, CA.

4   Demonstration Infant Program, directed with Tom Forrest, M.D., The Children's Health Council, Palo Alto, CA.

5   A residence for normal infants from birth to three years of age with a capacity to serve 70 infants, founded in 1946 by Emmi Pikler, M.D.

6   For a detailed description of the philosophy, methodology and the actual care of the infants at Loczy see (David and Appel, 1973).

7   Him or her. For simplicity's sake the infant is referred to as he, the carer as she.

pating each others' reactions fosters mutual understanding, acceptance and basic trust for both mother and child; thus, anticipation becomes the forerunner of communication. Selective intervention means knowing when not to intervene, and this is more difficult than intervening indiscriminately.

Our study was designed on the assumption that there are certain conditions under which a healthy, normal infant can develop his potential. They are as follows:

1. Availability of a mother figure who responds to physical and emotional needs.

2. Mother's correct perception and basic acceptance of the child — seeing and accepting him for what he is.

3. Synchronization of his inner rhythm (sleep, hunger, etc.) with the family's daily routine (mutual adaptation).

4. Availability of space (to facilitate locomotion).

5. Availability of objects (to facilitate manipulation).

6. Availability of other children within the same age range (to observe, imitate, interact and socialize with).[8]

In summary, our goals are influenced by our concept of an ideal human being as one who has some or many of the following characteristics: realistic trust in himself and his environment, perceptions of his inner needs and ability to communicate them, the ability to make choices for himself, which includes knowing and accepting the consequences of his choices, flexibiltity and the capacity to learn from past experiences, ability to deal actively with the present and plan for the future, free access to his creative talents and resources. Further, he is goal-oriented and also enjoys the process of problem-solving, whether physical, emotional, or cognitive. Identification with these ideals implies that we have to critically examine child-rearing practices in order to detemine which would facilitate and/or hinder the emergence of the desired characteristics in infancy.

Trust develops when the primary carers allow the child to anticipate what is going to happen to him. They must relate their trust in the infant and view him as an initiator of activities.

Infants do perceive their inner feelings and needs and learn to communicate them. Carers, however, when not sensitively observing the infant, do not respond to his communications, but rather to their own interpretations of the infant's needs. For example, a mother who is cold may cover the crying infant without trying to find out whether he is warm or cold.

---

[8] This condition is optional.

Making appropriate choices in life is a learning process lasting from birth to death. Few people realize at what an early age infants are able to make proper choices if given the opportunity. The carer has to differentiate between situations according to whether the infant has a real choice or not. If there is a real choice (e.g. "Do you want to be picked up now?"), and the child responds negatively or with disinterest, he is left alone. If no choice is involved, the carer does not ask, but states the intended action (e.g. "I am going to pick you up now. It is time to go.") The child is then picked up.

Flexibility of the body and mind develops throughout repeated exploratory exercises of infants in free play. Infants are not moving freely when they are restricted by mechanical devices such as infant seats, bouncers, walkers and swings, or encouraged to assume positions for which they are not yet ready. Propping up an infant into a sitting position before he can sit up or lie down by himself will not make him move better, become flexible or autonomous.

Infants do naturally have access to their own resources, unless we superimpose tasks which are beyond their capabilities.

It is truly fascinating to observe infants solving their own problems with concentration, endurance and good frustration tolerance. This happens if adults are available rather than intrusive, and if they learn to wait and see whether the child could work it out by himself before offering help. A freely exploring child "selects" his own problems and is internally motivated to solve them, in his own way, continuously learning without experiencing failure. Though some individual modifications are necessary when working with high-risk children, providing learning experiences without failure is even more important for them than it is for the average child.

While emphasizing the infant's need for autonomy, one must keep in mind the utmost importance of the relationship that the infant develops with his primary carer. An intimate, trusting relationship is the prerequisite for healthy separation and individuation of the child. Only after he gets "refueled" during the unhurried times he spends with his carer will he be willing to let go of the carer and explore his environment.

In this paper I have discussed infants' needs and adults' goals for them and suggested how to synchronize them. If our goal is an authentic individual, then we should let him be an authentic infant. Meeting the needs of infants is not an easy task for the family, and it becomes increasingly more difficult in various types of infant centers. Appropriate curriculum for infants should not be a special teaching plan added to their daily activities, but rather it should be incorporated in the infants' every experience. The types of programs offered, as well as curricula, should evolve as a joint effort between carers and infants. The carer provides space, objects and loving care; the infant explores the space, manipulates the objects, develops trust and self-confidence.

The guidelines for any and all intervention must be based on observation, empathy, sensitivity and respect for the infant.

REFERENCES

Bayley, N., <u>The Manual for the Bayley Scales of Infant Development</u>, Psychologi cal Corporation, 1969.

David, M., and G. Appel, <u>Loczy ou Le Maternage Insolite</u>, "Loczy: An Unusual Way of Caring," Translation by Gerber. Editions du Scarabee. Paris: Centres d'entrainement aux methods d'education active, 1973.

Gerber, M., "<u>Infants' Expression — The Art of Becoming</u>," Psychiatry and Art, edited by I. Jakab Karger. Basel, Switerland and New York, 1971, Vol. 3, 170-175.

Gesell, A., <u>Gesell Developmental Schedules</u>, Psychological Corporation, 1940.

Gordon, Ira J., <u>Baby Learning Through Baby Play: A Parents' Guide for the First Two Years</u>, Saint Martin: Griffin Series, 1970.

Painter, Genevieve, <u>Teach Your Baby</u>, N.Y.: Simon and Schuster, 1971.

Piaget, J., <u>The Origins of Intelligence in Children</u>, New York: W.W. Norton, 1963.

Pikler, E., "Learning of Motor Skills on the Basis of Self-Induced Movements," <u>Exceptional Infant Studies in Abnormalities</u>, 1971, 2.

Stone, L. Joseph and Henrietta Smith, (Lois B. Murphy Editors), <u>The Competent Infant</u>, N.Y.: Basic Books, 1973.

There are numerous articles, among them "The Gourmet Baby" in the January '83 issue of <u>California Magazine</u> and "Bringing Up Superbaby" in the March 28, '83 issue of <u>Newsweek</u>, which made my adrenalin flow when I read them.

While both articles seemingly share a common-sensical voice, by the very nature of mass-media reporting, the sensational gets more coverage and becomes more appealing than simple everyday living and coping with young children. While some people may respond to the voice of reason and begin to question what is really best for their infants, I fear many more will be lured by multicolored parachutes and flash cards of painters and brain parts. As a result, more and more babies will be tossed up in the air, put onto gymnastic equipment and taught irrelevant information, treated like objects and fed data like computers. I wonder if their trainers realize that time spent teaching the irrelevant deprives the child of time spent learning what would be relevant. It is like force-feeding the child with food he or she cannot digest.

David Elkind's excellent book, <u>Miseducation: Preschoolers at Risk</u>, addresses the real dangers of early education. In <u>The Self-Respecting Child</u> British educator Allison Stallibrass says, "A healthy human being has an appetite for the experience that will further the growth of his faculties. Given the opportunity, a baby spends most of his waking hours exercising his physical and mental faculties to the best of his ability. From birth he is motivated by a steady and persistent urge (that is only suspended for short intervals by the need for food, cuddling and sleep) to develop his latent ability to interact with his environment."

We believe that infants do what they can do — and should not be expected to do what they are not ready for. Infants constantly learn by taking in, finding out, discovering, integrating and organizing the real world around them. Knowledge gained this way will serve them best in their everyday lives. If only people would trust how perfectly babies are created, they could relax and enjoy all the daily miracles of natural development.

Parents are the first and the most important teachers of their children. But parents have gotten so busy and are trying so hard to "teach" their children that they do not realize just what the children are learning from them. Children who are taught to pick the "right" picture or give the "right" answer learn to please. They do not understand the questions, which have no meaning for them, so they cannot make a real choice; all they learn is to respond to their parent's cues. Parents may, even unintentionally, give clues such as facial expression, tone of voice or subtle gestures. Infants learn to perform, like an elephant in the circus who is not appreciated for just being an elephant, but for doing tricks.

How very sorry I feel for both the infants and their parents who are the unknowing victims of "gourmet" and "superbaby" fads. They do not realize the high price they may have to pay for their ambitious endeavors to speed up infancy and interfere with natural growth.

* From <u>Educaring</u>, Vol. IV, No. 2, Spring 1983.

FROM STRESS TO DISTRESS*

They may never connect early stressful training with problems frequently encountered later on: from sleeping and eating disorders to nervous and self-destructive behaviors (hair-pulling, nail-biting, stuttering, nervous tics, anorexia); from disinterested, bored and unmotivated students to early school dropouts and drug abusers.

While the effect of any environment is dependent on the child's personality, vulnerability and resilience, some of these children may need intensive psychotherapy at some point. But I have yet to hear of a single case in which a person (coming from loving parents and an average "expectable environment") sought therapy because he or she had not been taught enough during infancy.

The pendulum of child-rearing practices swings back and forth. Fads come and go quickly. But, as Sigmund Freud said, "The voice of the intellect is soft but persistent." We must be persistent if we want to help parents see the difference between what is universal and what is a changing fad in child-rearing, so that more infants may grow up into authentic children and adults. Although the "gourmet" and "superbaby" trainers make more noise, they will be long forgotten when the soft voice of reason will still be heard.

PART III:

FROM HUNGARY

EMMI PIKLER, M.D.

JUDIT FALK, M.D.

MARIA VINCZE, M.D.

A QUARTER
OF A
CENTURY OF
OBSERVING
INFANTS IN A
RESIDENTIAL
CENTER*

Establishing day care centers brings up many questions. For example: the kinds of children, the kinds of family backgrounds, how many hours per day and how many times per week, the age groupings, the staff ratio, and so on.

Before all these questions can be discussed, the most important one has to be faced: is it possible at all to care for children in groups, away from their families, without damaging them?

I believe I am able to contribute to this vital topic by relating my experiences based on a quarter of a century of working with infants in a residential institute.

The National Methodological Institute for Infant Care and Education, known as Loczy, was founded in 1946 for healthy children of mothers who died giving birth or who suffered from severe tuberculosis and whose families were not able to care for tiny infants. Seventy children, from birth to three years of age, live in our institute full time. Although many different methods are reported to be effective to date, the method we use, and find quite successful, is much different from the customary ones. Incidentally, it was very interesting to see how the basic principles of our work could be adapted to a very different setting by Magda Gerber in the Infant Project at the Dubnoff School.

Before going any further, I have to stress that by no means do we believe it is advantageous to rear infants away from their families. We wish all children would have families who could care for them. Only if this is not possible should the infant spend time in group care. But with or without a family, the infant still needs an intimate, stable, adult relationship, and that is the leading principle of infant care and education as practiced at Loczy. It is emphasized that what the child needs is not relationships with adults in general, but with the least possible number of certain stable adults. This is considered a necessary prerequisite for the healthy psychological and physical development of the infant. We emphasize that this social contact should be developed primarily during the various procedures of care.

But how can the infant nurse[1] give unhurried, individualized attention to each child within a group? — only if meanwhile the other infants are busily playing without adult help. This had to be arranged.

Accordingly, a satisfactory relationship between adult and child is formed primarily during the physical contacts, i.e., dressing, bathing, feeding, etc.,

by: Emmi Pikler
M.D., C.Sc.

---

* Presented at the Eighth Annual Joint Conference of the University of Southern California School of Medicine, Post Graduate Division, Dubnoff School for Educational Therapy, and Children's Hospital of Los Angeles on November 11, 1970 at the Ambassador Hotel in Los Angeles.

Care giver.

when the adult and child are in intimate personal contact. This is particularly true for the infant. It should be noted that most of the children are admitted to Loczy shortly after birth.

Simultaneously with building up the adult-child relationship, as an integral part of this, the adult systematically teaches the child all skills considered necessary under Loczy's educational principles. From the very beginning, the infant is encouraged to cooperate and increasingly participate in dressing, feeding, and bathing himself. The infant learns to listen (to a gradually increasing extent) to the words of the adult, to understand what he is expected to do, and to respond to the adult's wishes. At the same time, the infant nurse is able to notice the individual reactions of the infant and to respond to them. These responses in turn induce and promote the initiative of the infant and young child, his activity, and his speech.

On the other hand, our children have <u>never been taught</u> to perform certain skills which are generally taught. Loczy has encountered a great deal of criticism and controversy on this point. Yet we insist on continuing not to teach the children these skills.

What are the skills we refuse to teach our children? The infant is <u>never</u> put in a more advanced position, in order to promote gross motor development, than he is able to attain by himself from a basic supine position. His attention is never drawn to a toy by placing the toy in his hand, or having it dangle over his head, thus compelling him to notice it. Finally, we also make a point of not including social contact between the infants in conformity with adult ideas.

As a matter of principle, we refrain from teaching skills and activities which under suitable conditions will evolve through the child's own initiative and independent activity.

Naturally, <u>we</u> must provide the children suitable conditions — that is, freedom for activity and adequate space. Their environment must be stable, varied and colorful.

To achieve this, three to six infants over three months of age are kept together in very large play pens. The social contacts between these infants, their responses to each other, the sounds emitted, the movement surrounding them, all create a familiar and reassuring atmosphere, especially during the period when the infant nurse is caring for another child. The large size of the play pen area lessens the occurence of conflicting situations.

A good part of the children's play and nap time is spent outdoors, in the garden, where the natural surroundings offer continuous variety. They are given toys and other play material of <u>appropriate</u> quantity and quality, which they can use spontaneously, on their own initiative, without any danger to themselves or to each other. The children can peacefully, actively play together because they trust that an adult is always present and available. This means in practice that in all difficult or conflicting situations, unavoidably arising while the child is getting acquainted with the world, the adult should give immediate attention to the child who needs it.

Summarizing the experience of the first 24 years, we feel justly satisfied with the results achieved. On the whole, the children's development has been sound, and is similar to the pattern of development of children reared in families.

Hearing about children cannot be compared to actually seeing the children. Unfortunately I cannot invite all of you to come to Budapest and look at the children, as I would like to do.

Our positive evaluation of the Loczy children has been further supported by the 1964 survey of Hungarian researcher Margit Hirsch and her team. Thirty children, then aged three to nine years, who had been reared in their infancy in our Institute, and were later transferred back to their families, were selected at random. Psychologist Hirsch established that none of the children exhibited the symptoms of subsequent impairment generally considered typical of hospitalism.

At present, systematic re-examinations sponsored by a grant from the World Health Organization are being carried out on 100 children, now aged 16 to 24 years, reared in their infancy in Loczy and later in their families. Since these investigations are still in progress, the data gathered up till now cannot be evaluated as yet. The data is so far, however, very encouraging.

I have spoken about our methods and the good results in rearing infants, from their new-born period on, within the framework of an institute. If this is possible, then naturally, it must be easier to rear healthy infants in day care centers, where the children have to be separated from their families only part time.

But I have to stress that to meet the needs of infants in groups and out of their families is not an easy task. It works well only with professionals who are specially trained to work with children under three years of age, with suitable staff-infant ratio, adequate equipment, and plenty of room for the children, indoors and outdoors.

Specially trained supervisors are also needed to develop consistent, yet flexible and easily adaptable, daily schedules which are acceptable to the infants and which also facilitate the work of the caregivers.

I must emphasize that to run an infant program is quite different from, and cannot be based upon, well-known methods of operating schools or even nursery schools. Unfortunately, the topic of group care of infants is not yet fully elaborated, but at least it is now more recognized as a new science — a new field.

According to my experience in the U.S.A., now and five years ago during a former visit in your country, there is a growing desire to help children become healthy, happy, and well adapted adults. This desire will provide the impetus to overcome the numerous difficulties I have just described. I wish you great success in your future work.

CAN INFANT-CHILD CARE CENTERS PROMOTE OPTIMAL DEVELOPMENT?*

By: Emmi Pikler
M.D., C.Sc.

Beginning with the onset of the 20th century, pediatricians as well as psychologists have shown a growing interest in the psychic and somatic growth of infants and young children. It is remarkable that a broader and bolder reconsideration of traditional methods of infant care and education has nevertheless not taken place.

Some eminent researchers, directly observing infant development, such as Illingworth, Peiper and others, have examined infant development in outpatient departments, hospitals or clinics, either in sick children or children presented as suspect of illness, or those who came for a check-up. These examinations did not, of course, relate to precise data on the environment of these children in their homes.

Environment was taken into account only in broad, general outlines, if at all, even by authors like Bayley, Brunet-Lezine, Buhler-Hetzer, Figurine-Djenissova, Gesell-Amatruda and others who investigated the developmental patterning of normal healthy children in clinics or their homes. The same applies to observations made by certain researchers — pediatricians, biologists, psychologists, such as Piaget, Preyer, and Darwin who carefully observed and recorded the development of their own, or closely related, children. While these observations have furnished valuable data on the progression of infant development, yet even these significant works failed to include exact accounts of the educational environment. The same is true for Shirley's longitudinal observations on the development of 25 children. Here we get acquainted with generalized data on the development conditions and on the environment of the subjects, but the conventional practice of infant care is considered as an invariable factor by this author too; she neither investigates nor criticizes it.

At this point I should like to quote Whiting and Whiting. These anthropoligists say: "If children are studied within the confines of a single culture, many events are taken as natural, obvious, or a part of human nature and are therefore not reported and not considered as a variable. It is only when it is discovered that other people do not follow these practices that have been attributed to human nature, that they are accepted as variables."

Apparently, all the above-mentioned researchers also considered their particular educational circumstances "natural" or "obvious."

Some of these researchers set up development schedules on the psychological and somatic development of infants and young children, based upon the behavioral patterns found by them in the majority of the healthy infants

---

* Presented at the Eighth Annual Joint Conference of the University of Southern California School of Medicine, Post Graduate Division, Dubnoff School for Educational Therapy, and Children's Hospital of Los Angeles on November 14, 1970 at the Ambassador Hotel in Los Angeles.

observed. The developmental schedules so established have generally been considered as psychological. They have become standards or norms.

This standard has been expected from the healthy, normally developing infants by parents, teachers, and advisors. These expectations have fixed the conventional methods of care and education, those which, in turn, brought about the expected pattern of development.

The circle is thus closed. Observations carried out without accurate analysis of environmental factors were instrumental in stabilizing the accepted conventional methods of infant care.

Since, however, conventional infant care differs to a greater or lesser extent — by continents, by countries and even by groups of people — obviously the developmental patterns observed under dissimilar educational conditions, and the norms derived from them, are also dissimilar.

The ways and means of reassessment by experiments are greatly limited since it is obviously <u>impermissible</u> to bring up infants or young children under potentially harmful experimental conditions.

Thus, we can't state today what should be considered as optimal development in infancy. Consequently, I cannot answer the question which is the title of my speech — whether infant-child care centers can promote optimal development. All I can do in order to evaluate results is to compare the development of infants raised in a center to the development of infants raised in families within the same culture.

I have spoken about my experiences of a quarter of a century with young children under three years of age reared in the National Methodological Institute for Infant Care and Education (popularly called Loczy) in Budapest under full time residential care. I have reported that the children's development proved to be favorable, that is, they develop, by and large, normally — similarly to children reared in average families.

I want to emphasize that not only do we give attention and care, we also <u>expect</u> the infant's active participation and cooperation.

As you will see, from the newborn period on, we keep in mind our goals to guide infants to become self reliant and independent. But here I have to stop and clarify.

When I say independent, I mean independent in choosing and using a toy, in moving any way he wants to, in using his play time as he pleases, to become gradually more and more independent in feeding, clothing, and bathing himself... I do <u>not</u> mean that we want our children to become independent of, or unrelated to, the adults who rear them or the society they live in. On the contrary, we expect our children to accommodate better and better, to respond to the respect of other children, to cooperate with the adults and to become creative, active members of society.

FORMS OF HOSPITALISM IN OUR DAYS

Emmi Pikler
M.D., C.Sc.
1975

The subject of my paper is a group of "hospitalism" symptoms wherein the impairment of the children does not appear in a strikingly negative form.

The institutions for rearing healthy young children under three years in Hungary, as well as this type of institute all over the civilized world, have seen an enormous development during this century. The hospitalism syndrome which previously resulted in the death of the majority of children, and was observed by Pfaundler in the early years of the 20th century in young children left to stay in the hospital after recovery, later by Spitz in infants reared in residential institutions for healthy children, now belongs to the past. In most of these institutions the children now survive, although accurate surveys show their mortality rate to be higher all over the world, including this country, than the average rate of the age group.

As a result of the survival of infants reared in institutions, a new problem has emerged from the 1950's on relating aberrations in the adult personality to development patterns of institutionally reared children. Based on data collected by him in various parts of the world, commissioned by WHO, Bowlby (1951: p. 31; 1957: pp. 34-37) found that most of the persons deprived of their families in their early years displayed special personality disorders, appearing primarily in the superficiality of social contacts, in difficulties of affect control, and occasionally in restricted cognitive and perceptive functions.

Since these late personality disorders appear even in children who were returned to their families after the first, second or third institutional years, these early years seem to be primarily responsible for the said disorders. Similar observations were made by Hirsch (1961) in her follow-up study made in Hungary.

Bowlby (1951: p. 95) stresses — among other things — that persons reared institutionally during infancy are apt to become criminal, antisocial elements and enter into indiscriminate sexual relations, as a result of their personality traits. The women give birth to children irresponsibly and don't care for their children, just as their parents failed to care for them, whereby they continue to increase the number of abandoned children.

What can we expect from the population now being reared in residential nurseries, after they have grown up? What is the present day situation in our nursery homes?

There is a growing number of institutions in this country where the children are no longer remarkably pale, and most of them are neither depressed nor inactive, as was generally experienced in the past. In these institutions one can hardly find a child who would spend his day practicing stereotyped movements. Most of the children have rather cheerful expressions, they play with toys in their hands, they move about, they seem to coexist peacefully, even in restricted space; they welcome the adult's approach, and enjoy being held in the adult's arms. By the age of three, the majority of these infants are able to dress more or less alone, to eat alone, they are toilet trained and can also speak. They are largely similar to children of their age group raised in the family. It is true they are somewhat backward in almost all areas of psychomotor development, and they contract illnesses substantially more often than family reared children; their morbidity rate is higher than even in day-nurseries, although their environment is more separated, more infection proof. This points at their reduced resistance. Yet all this is not prominent, it does not strike the casual observer.

Numerous insitutions are not yet up to this standard. At this time, however, I will not deal with the problems for children in the poorly run institutions. I am now conerned with the problems arising in the better ones, where, however misleading the children's behavior in the comparatively well-run institutions may be at first glance, most of these children are severely impaired in their personality development. Unless further changes occur, we must expect Bowlby's pattern to appear in the future.

What makes us worry about the children's state, in spite of the improvements just described?

In most of the relatively well-run institutions, there is a striking, almost total absence of volitional activity and of initiative in children of otherwise fairly sound overall state, children who at first glance make a good impression.

The children, as a rule, play what they are told or shown by the adult, in the way they are instructed to. Frequently one can see groups of children around two years of age playing with identical sets of building blocks, handling the blocks the same way. If the string of a toy is placed in their hand, and they are told to pull it, they will pull the toy. If the toy gets upset, they will wail and wait for the adult to set it right, so that they may continue pulling. If they are asked to, they will line up; if they are put in sitting position, they will generally remain so. No individual manifestations, no personal initiative will disturb the guiding work of the adult. As a rule, they refrain from touching what they are not allowed to touch; in some of the group playrooms of our residential nurseries, one can occasionally find open shelves housing more or less dangerous objects which the children could easily reach by climbing on a chair, yet they make no such attempt, even though the chair is there.

In the street, they will follow the adult by age two; they will not run off or stop to look, and will not take an active interest in what is happening in the street. Hence, a large number of children can be walked by a small number of adults.

The child is a puppet in the adult's hand, who will act upon definite instructions, by no means on his own initiative. Children who are able to sit steadily will accept food in a passive lying position, their arms dangling, until the adult decides to seat them in a chair or bench, giving the spoon in their hands and instructing them to eat alone.

These children can be dressed in garments of any color or shape, they have no relationship to colors and shapes, although they are able to sort out colors if asked to do so.

Older children, when they are not told what to do, sometimes loiter about aimlessly, waiting for guidance from the adult. They appear to live in a fog, groping about in an unfamilar world without even trying to familiarize themselves with it or get their bearings. The children have no personal relationship with their way of living, nor with the surrounding world of objects, and are hardly aware of their own bodies. The adult may pick them up, and then put them down, either back to their initial place, or somewhere else, in the cot or in the playpen, perhaps somewhere else, practically without the children's noticing it. At the same time they are eager to reproduce things and can be readily taught to carry out certain tasks upon instructions.

The volitional acts of these children, even the negative ones, are extremely scarce, and hardly reminiscent of the manifestation of family reared children. As an example, I would describe the feeding of a group of eight 10 to 14 month-old children. Our observations cover a case where the children did not like the food they were given. They began eating regularly, subsequently opened their mouths less and less, turning the food in their mouths longer and longer before swallowing it. Even though they definitely disliked the food, they kept on opening their mouths for some time when told so, and only when they were completely disgusted did they begin to wail softly and miserably. Yet even then, their lips were so slack that the nurse was able to shove in the spoon without a particular effort. This is a typical kind of behavior, often observed. Only one single baby, aged 10 months, reacted in a different way. As soon as feeding was started, not liking the food in his mouth, he shut his lips tightly, averted his head and when offered another spoonful, he pushed away the caretaker's arm holding the spoon. That child had been transferred to the institute only two days ago, for his mother had been taken suddenly ill.

In reaction to a grave conflict which arose in them to the extent that they were overwhelmed with passion and thus unable to obey the adult's instructions, some of the older children flung themselves prostrate to the ground, as if embracing the floor, without uttering a sound or word. This kind of protest reaction was only observed in institutional children. A family-reared child may occasionally go into tantrums, throw himself forward full length, but he will always insist on communicating to the adult his protest; he will shriek, rave, kick about, make a scene. The children we observed in the institute acted differently; they lay low like an insect sensing danger, as if struck to the ground.

In addition to the lack of acts of volition, another characteristic feature is the impersonality of the child's relationship to the adult. Any attendant may pick them up, put them down, feed them, may put a toy in their hands or withdraw it, without meeting the child's opposition. In those institutes where adults treat the infants and children with uniform, overall routine kindness, the children enjoy being picked up, they smile, without, however, looking at the adult's face or in his eyes. They are pleased, not because a beloved person took them in her arms — they hardly care who picks them up —, but because they enjoy the warmth of being hugged in someone's arms.

The impersonality of relations, the lack of the children's interest in their own bodies and their own needs become even more apparent during care. Practically from the newborn period onwards, caretaking offers manifold chances for interactions between the young child and the adult, for giving countless indications of getting acquainted with each other, and for the child to get familiar with his own body. Yet in the majority of institutions, the infants are totally passive during care. While they are being dressed or undressed they remain in the position in which they were first placed on the dressing table. A baby already able to turn around and move freely may be left on the dressing table for a while, and he may not budge. A child already able to stand and walk may be laid on the table like a rag doll, with his arms and legs dangling; he may be dressed or undressed without any sign of cooperation or, for that matter, resistance. You may put something on or take something off of the baby, or wash him in a moment's time. It may happen that the children are cheerful and pleased, or laugh during these operations of care, and the adult may occasionally talk. All this, however, occurred in an entirely unrelated manner, without the adult and the child watching each other, or responding to one another. These actions of care lack cooperation, there is no action-reaction character of the occurrences; mutual interest is not necessary, and there is no personal relationship between the child and the adult tending him.

The behavior of a baby of unimpaired personality reared by an affectionate mother is entirely different. A healthy, properly developing infant or young child is characterized by practically unremitting initiative. He will not keep quiet for a minute while he is on the dressing table, he will bounce, turn, make various attempts; when undressed, he will enjoy being naked, later he will try to get acquainted with his own body, and take hold of everything within his reach. He will get to the edge of the dressing table in a moment, and try to see what is below him. In accordance with his degree of maturity he will taste things or throw them away, he will keep on experimenting; he cannot be left on the dressing table by himself for a minute. In the second half year of life the infant will initiate play. He will glide away, turn away or wriggle off the diapers in the last minute, laughing at his mother.

The healthy infant and young child expects to be dressed and bathed according to his own natural schedule, even according to his own pace. If these are not adhered to, he will cry and protest. He keeps on watching his mother's expression and responds to it; eventually when his mother loses patience, the baby will stop fooling, or become unhappy.

Mother and child know each other and their habits. They respond sensitively to each other's various manifestations and live them as a common experience. Dressing, undressing or bathing the baby gives rise to more and more interactions, and claims more and more time.

The healthy, unimpaired infant very soon distinguishes his mother from other adults. Perhaps he will not suffer to be fed by someone else, he may cry when picked up by a stranger, or at least stare at him with interest. He will not respond to the caresses or petting of a stranger with the same sweet smile that he does when fondled by his mother, his father or some other close adult, or a brother or a sister he is fond of. The baby's bond to his mother therefore means more than merely a welcome, agreeable stimulation of the skin, or enfolding of arms. They involve a great many interactions and shared pleasure, where the baby is not simply the object of an activity but also an active partner who adds new initiatives in his own way, and is intent on realizing his own will, to achieve his own desires. He needs, in this ongoing process, to be understood and helped by the adult. This often leads to conflicts. The child living in the family is jealous of his brother or sister or he may perhaps be jealous of his father, not because he is "not well behaved," but because he is fond of his mother and is angry with everyone and everything that may divert her attention.

No trace of this behavior can be observed in institutionally reared children.

A child reared in the family will later try out things on his own initiative. During the "I, Myself" or "self, self" stage he learns how to stick to his own will and to adjust actively to the adult way of life. The basis of his adjustment is that he wants to become a grown-up person; he will gradually want to adopt, accept and assimilate the requirements raised by the affectionate parents. He wants to act and behave accordingly, even if he does not always succeed.

This again cannot be observed in institutional children.

The above described state of the children — currently observed in residential nurseries — is considered by us a novel, not yet described syndrome of hospitalism. This syndrome is characterized by the fact that, while certain glaringly negative traits no longer appear in the child's development state and comportment, the fundamental personality disorders are not eliminated.

Is it possible to anticipate the formation of this syndrome and, if so, how?

The best solution would be based on the moral and material assistance of the public. The necessity of residential institutions could be reduced in the future, and the number of children reared outside the family home, deprived of a loving parent, could be lessened. However, the need for institutions will continue to exist, and even though the institutes will not be able to rear the child at the same level as can be done in the family, we have to stress that the conditions outlined above do not necessarily follow from institutional education, but can be ascribed to certain shortcomings in the work of these institutions.

The point is that it is possible to rear children institutionally with an improved personality development pattern, and this is confirmed by the twenty-seven years of experience in the Loczy institute, as well as by the results of the follow-up study sponsored by the WHO, directed to children formerly placed at the Loczy Institute. These were discussed in a recent issue of <u>Magyar Pszichologiai Szemle</u>.

The task is not an easy one and cannot be achieved unless certain material, objective and personnel conditions are fulfilled. Yet these conditions are available in a fairly large portion of Hungarian institutes, or if they are not, their fulfillment is under way.

This is, however, not the main difficulty; what is more important is to put an end to the impersonal, casual, routine kindness and to all forms of drill, even in its seemingly attractive forms. In order to achieve a more healthy personality development, we must take pains to build up a closer human relationship, based on cooperation beginning at infancy and a relationship resembling the one evolving in families. As a result, the child will follow the request or instruction issued by the adult, not because he has no independent will, but because sound, reciprocal, close human relationship and cooperation lead to a social adjustment pattern, where the children find their environment satisfying their particular interests in the young community and preparing them to participate in future communities. The children will cooperate in such a manner as to be able to shape their future lives by establishing a balance between their individual and community interests. All this cannot be realized without a profound transformation in the approach of caretakers as well as the people controlling and supervising the institutions.

The problem is all the more difficult for the staff of residential nurseries, since they are accustomed to tend passive, moldable children of aberrated personalities, who have no will of their own, and may be guided like a flock under the guise of education. The caretakers therefore have no experience in the guidance of groups of young children having an age-appropriate will, whose development and interest are normal, who have age-appropriate personalities and initiatives. The educational attitude based on active adjustment of the child resulting in genuine social adjustment is strange to these educators.

Another impediment to the adults' readiness to change their attitudes is that a more advanced way of life in the institutes, a change for the better will not promptly produce conspicuous results, nor will it make the population of the nurseries easier to manage. On the contrary, as a result of better educational work the children become more difficult to manage in certain respects. They become less quiet, the number of conflicts will increase, supervision must be closer, they call for increased attention. A good many routine methods of care and organization must be discontinued. For example, if the children become more active under better conditions, two adults will no longer be sufficient for taking 12, or even more, young children for a walk in a busy street, nor will the attendant be able to leave the infant alone on the dressing table during a diapering. Various pieces of furniture and implements will have to be changed, because they will become hazardous when the children's behavior becomes normal, when their activity, initiative and enterprising mood increase. Hence, the expectations raised for the child will have to be modified in relation to present day expectations; the inner life and organization of the institution, as well as the evaluation of results, will have to be transformed accordingly.

I'd like to call attention to another difficulty which must not be underestimated. It is hard to convince those who have put great effort and serious work to eliminating the visible evidence of past mistakes — the remarkably poor state of the children—and who have achieved results that were deemed to be good. It is difficult to combat their complacency, to make them see that further progress is necessary and to make them realize that in spite of all appearances, the children are impaired in their personalities.

We must confess that if we had not repeatedly witnessed it, we ourselves would not have believed possible the controversial pattern of personality development produced in some of our institutions.

What we found most alarming is that hospitalized children formerly used to be remarkably different from the family raised children in their appearance, development pattern and attitudes; as long as these children were pale and idle, rocking themselves all day long, as long as they aroused pity and consternation, both the professional and the non-professional observer were fully aware that one could not, and should not, resign oneself to this situation. The present situation, on the other hand, gives rise to unjustified satisfaction, even complacency and pride over the results achieved.

This is why we considered as particularly dangerous the novel form of the hospitalism syndrome evolved in this country as well as in many other places, occurring especially in the well-equipped, aspiring institutions.

Bowlby, J., <u>Maternal Care and Mental Health</u>, Geneva: World Health Organization, 1951.

Bowlby, J., <u>Child Care and the Growth of Love</u>, Penguin Books: London, 1957, p. 34-47.

Spitz, R.A., "Hospitalism: An Inquiry into the Genesis of Psychiatric Conditions in Early Childhood," <u>Psychoan. Study of the Child</u>, 1945, p. 53.

REFERENCES

DEVELOP-MENTAL SCHEDULES STIMULATING ADULT EDUCATIONAL ATTITUDES

Judit Falk, M.D.

Every method, set of standards, or developmental schedule has a direct or indirect effect on the educator who is acquainted with the data or requirements contained in them. Hence, the phases of development recorded in these sets of standards or test schedules elaborated as a rule for diagnostic development are often considered as educational aims — in most cases disregarding, or in contrast to, the original intentions of the authors who had set up these tables. Some users of these test tables, however, find this situation not only natural, but even desirable.

Other authors have elaborated dual-purpose tables or schedules based on the usual test questions. On one hand they are used for controlling development, and, on the other hand, the data of the schedules constitute aims to be achieved by the adult who handles and tends the child or infant.

We have been working for the last few years in our Institute on elaborating a control method which is suitable for exerting a direct, frank and purposeful influence on the attitude of the nurse, in the direction we consider desirable. The principles underlying our methods have been disclosed in 1964 in "Nepegeszsegugy" Public Health, Budapest, and the tables based on these principles have been published in "Gyermekgyogyaszat" Pediatrics, Budapest in 1968, as well as the XVIth International Congress of Applied Psychology, Amsterdam, 1968.

Our tables should not be regarded as a psychodiagnostic examination method. They are not intended to be used as a means of providing information on the neurological maturity or the highest achievements or capabilities of the child. Our recordings do not register phenomena observed in test situations. They record behavioral patterns repeatedly observed in the infants day by day, and recurrently during the day. In other words, what we intend to control is not what the infant is able to perform in structured situations conforming to test requirements — we wish rather to get acquainted with the activities recurrently practiced by the child in his daily life, while playing or being tended, for his own pleasure, on his own initiative.

The recordings of the patterns and progress of the child's activities serves as a means for evaluating the educational impact of the environment, but, at the same time, the recording acts also on the adult, the nurse, who is the most important element of the educational environment. It should be noted that the notes are taken by the nurse herself, and not by a special control person. Accordingly, the nurse is directly influenced by the questions of the table as to what manifestations she should expect from the child. The expectations of the nurse, in turn, influence the child both directly and indirectly. The direct influence consists in her approval, her joy shown on experiencing the expected activity. The indirect influence is perhaps still more important; she will create the optimum circumstances and she will handle and tend the child in a manner enabling him to produce, to practice the activities she has been expecting and which she is going to record. We have been obviously trying to record the manifestations, behavioral patterns and activities which appear recurrently, only in a psychically balanced state of the child.

Our table is based on a total of 100 questions. They cover four main aspects of the child's manifestations and development. Nearly one third of the questions relate to the child's comportment while being tended, more than one third relate to sound and speech development, while another third refers to the development of gross motor and manipulation activities.

The impact of the questions on the attitude of the nurse can be demonstrated by means of the questions relating to the child's comportment while being tended.

The first question in connection with bathing is whether the child is relaxed or not. If the nurse endeavors to answer in the affirmative, then she must handle the child in such a manner that the young infant, who responds by an increase in muscular tonus to any change in his state of equilibrium and to any sudden tactile stimulus, be spared from any such stimuli. In order that the infant admitted at the age of 2 or 3 weeks, and quite often not so handled previously, shall cease to be in tension during the various phases of cleaning, bathing and drying, the nurse has to handle him with extremely gentle and careful movements. Only as a next step can the nurse set herself the aim of the infant's relative cooperation, which is the second point. To secure such cooperation, the operations of care have to be performed in precisely the same manner and must very strictly follow the same sequence, even for the slightest details, in the case of each nurse. Only in this way can the nurse produce a situation where the child adapts, gets used to and expects the various phases of the bathing operation. The next stage of development, splashing in the water, can only be attained if bathing becomes a pleasant, joyous part of the daily routine, if beyond mere cleaning, bathing turns into a happy, intimate infant-adult contact, where the adult performs his task with warmth and pleasure, instead of a mechanical, impersonal manner.

The subsequent questions of the table have a similar effect. The infant will put out his leg and arm to be washed, soaped or dried, if he is repeatedly asked to and expected to do so. He will initiate play if he is given the time and opportunity, if the nurse does not become impatient when the baby unexpectedly turns prone or kicks off the diaper when he is almost completely diapered, if the nurse, on the contrary, shares with the baby the fun of undressing, bathing, dressing and diapering a restless, bouncing baby. Only a child who finds fun in being undressed, dressed, or bathed can be expected to perform some and increasingly more parts of these operations by himself. If the nurse fails to allow the child the time he needs for satisfying his attempts at independence, then there will not be satisfactory results for her to record in the corresponding columns. The same is true for other fields of care, and for eating habits: the child will only exhibit endeavors at self-dependence, if his active participation is allowed, encouraged and promoted by the nurse.

We assign particular significance to the questions on sound and language development. Special sets of questions in this category are concerned with the infant's response to adult talk, his initiating talk, sound forming, his verbal expression and his grammar. In connection with the first set of questions the nurse is not instructed to address the child either during or apart from care, but to observe and record how the child reacts — in various situations — to the nurse's talk. Evidently she has to address the baby to this end, and in such a way as to permit him to respond in an increasingly advanced manner. This is how infants aged 4-6 weeks come to fix their gaze on the speaker's face, those aged 5-9 weeks begin to form sounds with their lips, those aged 6-12 weeks respond by sound, and those aged 10-19 weeks respond by continual cooing. If the nurse comments on each stage of care in such a manner as to attract and maintain the child's attention, then she will be able to record for almost every 6 to 9 month old that he understands, by the speech and situation together, what he is expected to do. Incidentally, if the nurse would like to record at the end of the first year, or at the beginning of the second, that the child comprehends some adult language outside the care situations, then she has to talk to him attentively and consistently, also apart from care. In order that the nurse be able to record that the 18 to 24 month olds understands what is communciated to them, she has to state constantly in so many words what she wants them to do, to trust the children to understand her and to wait until they actually do what she wishes.

One of the major reasons why institutional children as a rule lag far behind in understanding adult speech is that the environment yields little reward for their response. In addition to this initial failure to observe the responses properly, in the next phase the adult quite often will not wait until the child does what he is asked to, thus checking his verbal comprehension: when the child is told to sit down, often he is promptly made to sit down; when he is told to go somewhere, he is taken by the hand, pulled or pushed; if he is asked to pass an object to the adult, it is instantly taken out of his hands, and very often all this is done without even uttering a word. In other words, the adult rarely waits until the child carries out what he is supposed to. The child so treated may perhaps understand the intonation of an order, but he will not really comprehend the words themselves. He will turn "responsive," docile, without actually understanding verbal address.

The fact that the environment does not pay sufficient attention and does not respond appropriately to the child's sounds, his speech initiative, his preverbal and verbal expression, is one of the major reasons why institutional children are often retarded in using langauage. If, however, the nurse is supposed to regularly record these manifestations, then she will follow them and respond to them with increased interest, this being the preliminary condition to meet and be able to record manifestations of a more and more advanced stage. Moreover, she will encourage the child to use verbal expression beyond mere reproduction to communciate his requests, thoughts, or emotions, if the child feels and realizes that he is listened to, that his communications or wishes are responded to.

If we want the nurse to devote so much attention to each child, the children must be able to spend the rest of their waking time — beyond the periods of care and of personal contact with the nurse — in happy activities. They must be provided with ample room for gross motor functions, manipulation, and play. Such a situation, however, can only be produced if certain objective conditions are fulfilled, in addition to the child's inner urge based on his emotionally balanced state.

If the nurse wants to record in her schedule good results for gross motor activities, manipulation and play, then she will see that the chldren have ample room available and that they actually spend their waking time there, that their clothes are unrestrictive, that toys fitting their age level are available in sufficient quantity and quality. She will make the active, playful children feel assured of receiving aid and protection whenever they meet unexpected, unpleasant situations or if they feel uncomfortable.

It is almost impossible to keep apart the conditions conducive to progress in the various areas of development. They require an overall educational attitude which relies on and encourages the child's feeling of security, his active mood and interest, due to his inner urge. Our schedules stimulate and encourage this kind of educational attitude, thus contributing active aid and real support to the achievement of one of our major aims: that the mechanical, impersonal, often impatient comportment of the nurses which constitutes a still persisting danger in day and residential nurseries, be replaced by a thorough and exact observation of the child, and by an increasingly sensitive response to his personality and requirements.

REFERENCES

Cattel, P., <u>The Measurement of Intelligence of Infants</u>, New York: Psychological Corporation New York, 1940.

Frankenburg, W.K. and J.B. Dodds, "The Denver Developmental Screening Test," <u>J. of Pediatrics</u>, 1967, 71, 181-191.

Gesell, A. and C.S. Amatruda, <u>Developmental Diagnosis</u>, New York: Harper and Row Inc., 1964.

The age (in percentiles) in which the manifestations of the activity belong to the everyday life

The age (in percentiles) in which the manifestations of the activity belong to the everyday life

EXAMINATION
OF THE
SOCIAL
CONTACTS OF
INFANTS
AND YOUNG
CHILDREN
REARED
TOGETHER

Maria Vincze,
M.D.

The social contacts of infants and young children have been investigated by Ch. Buhler, Sandler and Lictenberger. Lictenberger dealt with the social contacts of his own twins in their first years, Sandler examined the social contacts between children aged 1 to 2 years, brought up in an institute, while Ch. Buhler's investigations relate to social contacts between pairs of children who were associated for the purpose of examination. Provence and Lipton, also Meierhofer and Keller described in detail their experience with children reared in various American and Swiss institutes, but they devote only cursory attention to their social contacts.

The bulk of what one can read in textbooks of psychology on the social contacts of the age group in question is based on Buhler's examinations. These examinations, however, have been performed under quite special conditions; accordingly, her results are only valid for that particular situation. In fact, her examinations took place in an outpatient clinic, so that the situation was unusual for the children themselves. They did not know each other. The pairs she examined were composed of children of similar as well as different ages; they belonged to the age group of 4 to 22 months, but were mostly 6 to 12 months. The infants were made to sit up in small cots, facing each other at arm's length. Various toys were offered to one or both of them. In these age groups, particularly in the 6th to 12th months, known as "Greifalter" (the age of grasping) — new, unfamiliar objects are extremely attractive. The presentation of a new toy is a challenge for the child to grab it, to enter into a conflict, but it does not induce contacts; experiments carried out under such conditions are suitable for throwing light upon the formation and trend of a conflict situation rather than investigating the pattern of social contacts.

The situation contained a number of elements which were responsible for Buhler's results, where antagonism was much more frequently experienced than intimate association. Among these elements we mention the sitting posture of children who were not able to sit by themselves, and the resulting feeling of uncertainty and helplessness, also the impossibility of locomotion, the unfamiliar environment and strange partner, and the challenge of a new toy. All these factors may have contributed to Buhler's setting up the categories of "overlord and underdog," of the gestures of tyrant and subject.

We are not aware of any publications on investigations of social contacts in groups of young children and infants reared together. This is the more peculiar, as the number of very young children brought up together in day nurseries as well as residential ones shows an increasing trend throughout the world. Education in groups at such a young age raises numerous problems, both in regard to the theory of personality development and to educational practice. Nevertheless, the interrelations of institutionally reared infants and young children have not been investigated, perhaps in view of the difficulties involved. It should be noted that such investigations can only be carried out under certain conditions, such as:

1. The children's emotional pattern must be appropriate; they must have a firm, warm relationship with their nurse. Only children whose nurse laughs at, talks to and plays with them, can be expected to laugh back at their nurse and will laugh at and play with their peers. It is not by chance that for the children reared in the American institute investigated by Lipton and Provence, where the nurses treated the children in a cool and impersonal manner, the examiners found hardly any special contacts between the children, for example no peek-a-boo at all, since the children had next to no adult emotional contacts.

2. Beyond being reared in a group, the children must spend their waking times together in large playpens. If the children spend their days in separate cots, screened off from each other by bars, they are greatly inhibited in developing social contacts of some variety.

3. To carry out longitudinal examinations, i.e., to follow up children from the age of 3 months to 2 and 1/2 years, it is necessary for the group to remain constant in composition, even if transferred to some other places.

4. In order to examine the phenomena proper, and not the direct influence of the adult, a situation which renders Sandler's observations difficult to evaluate, a certain reserve on the part of the nurse is essential. This applies to the guidance she gives the children in play, since children will play together even without any adult guidance at all, and to her interference in the conflicts between children, since most of the conflicts will be straightened out without adult interference.

For evaluating the examinations, it is important to be well acquainted with the environment, the educational conditions and methods. It is not certain that any or all of the phenomena will be produced if the circumstances are different. Different conditions of examination, different educational circumstances may produce dissimilar phenomena — perhaps less, perhaps more.

All these conditions have been available in our Institute so that a longitudinal examination could be readily performed.

The age of the subjects ranged from 3 months to 30 months at the end. The greatest age difference — between the oldest and youngest child in the group — was 6 months. The group comprised 9 children most of the time; this number fell to 6 to 5 in the last few months.

Two to three 15-minute records a week were written on the children's play time. The scene of the observations was the large common pen or a compartment of a room in the first year and a half, and later the day nursery itself and the garden.

The method of examination, the technique employed by Merei in his small group experiments, is actometric recording. In other words, the patterns of behavior characteristic of the individual children were recorded verbally during our examinations, and so were the interactions of the children, and the events taking place among them. In recording, a three part scheme has been followed: the processes were classified as action, reaction and counter-action. This three part classification indicates what sorts of reactions may be expected to certain actions, and, similarly, what counter-actions. We were chiefly interested in finding out how the reaction to actions involving sensations of physical pain or inconvenience to a peer influenced the subsequent behavior of the active party; whether he realized, and at what stage, the discomfort or pain caused, and if so, whether this realization had any effect on his subsequent behavior.

The social interrelations we observed were grouped into 7 categories, on the basis of our preliminary examinations performed on children of various age groups. The longitudinal examinations were begun working with these 7 categories. In the course of the examination it appeared necessary to introduce two further categories, and the original 7 ones have also been modified. The social interactions were grouped under the following headings:

1. Contact by look, smile, sound

2. Initiation of contact by gesture or locomotion

3. Physical contact

4. Taking an object away

5. Offering — giving something

6. Imitation/acts performed together

7. Common activities, acts performed together

8. Verbal communication

9. Simulate adult attitudes towards peer

Each category comprises a number of different actions, of which we shall enumerate a few examples. Any unintentional touch or palpation — whether connected with a gesture, movement or with an object — has been classified as physical contact and so were all intentional, manipulative, explorative palpations, kind or rude gesture-like moves, such as caressing, hitting, kicking or biting, also beating peer with an object. Also included in this category were actions involving gross motor activities, such as climbing or scrambling onto peer. "Blind" offering, i.e., offering an object to a child who was not prepared to take it, or even turned his back on the offering party, was classified as "giving-offering." The same applies to a number of other actions, like holding out to a peer's eyes; later apparently intentional hoaxing of a peer by holding the object out to him. Other actions classified under the same heading include the intentional or unintentional transmittal of an object to a peer by shoving, rolling, or otherwise placing the object next to or in front of him; forceful giving, i.e., pressing an object into the peer's hand; also the act of showing an object to a peer. Actions like returning to the original owner an object previously lost or taken away from him; offering something to a peer instead of an object which had been thrown away or lost; offering to a peer an object recently taken away from another child; actions by which a child contributed to the playing activity of a peer, for example by offering or adding an object to a construction of a peer, were also included — under various subheadings — in the category of "giving-offering."

Each action, reaction or counter-action was indicated by a separate code, totaling 260. We have no space here for a detailed description of the categories. We merely mention that quite often one phenomenon is apt to be classified into a number of categories. All other categories could come under our 7th category, that of "common activities." This particular category, incidentally, does not show the three part composition of the rest.

The working up of the results of these examinations is still under way. The method and some of the experiences gathered during the first phases have been published. An account of the pattern of the seventh category — that of common activities — will be given in the future.

As to our results, we merely point out that they are not in full conformity with Buhler's nor with those of the various textbooks based on Buhler.

In fact, in the subjects under examination — which conformed to the age group 6 to 12 monthers mainly investigated by Buhler — we also found that most of the children's contacts were established by means of objects, and that within this category the act of taking objects away occurred quite frequently. Nevertheless, this age group is not characterized by a large number of conflicts; the social interrelation of the children seems to offer considerably more pleasure than discontentment. We have found that while the dictatorial and subject types, the overlord and the underdog, as described by Buhler do appear as behavioral patterns, the roles were interchanged, even within the framework of one observation. Finally, we were able to record a substantially broader, more lively and colorful range of social contacts than those recorded by Buhler in the experimental situation.

Our data seems to be closer to the pattern of the social contacts as recorded by Lichtenberger, based on his observations of his own twins.

Buhler, Ch., <u>Die ersten sozialen Verhaltungsweinsen des Kindes,</u> Fischer <u>Verlag</u>, Jena; 1927; p. 102.

Lichtenberger, W., <u>Mitmenschiliches Verhaltens eines Zwillingspaares in seinen ersten Lebensjahren</u>, Munich: Ernest Reinhardt Verlag, 1965, p. 48.

Provence, S. and R.D. Lipton, <u>Infants in Institutions</u>, New York: International Universities Press, 1962. p. 191.

THE IMPORTANCE OF PERSON-ORIENTED ADULT-CHILD RELATIONSHIPS AND BASIC CONDITIONS THERETO

Judit Falk, M.D.

In one of her studies, Margaret Mead relates an experience regarding the reactions of the same audiences to which the Spitz, Aubry and Robertson films were shown in succession. The reactions elicited by the first two films were different from those triggered by the third. The Spitz and Aubry films show the behavior of institutional children who suffered grave hospitalism, whereas the Robertson film deals with the reactions of a child aged two years, transferred suddenly from his home environment to a hospital for a few days. Mead states that the first two films are viewed with compassion and consternation, whereas the third film elicits a protest reaction, since what is shows "may happen to our children too." Mead adds we must always remember the very real difference that exists between professional, impersonal ethics, and ethics based on personal motivation. The former carries the message: "no single child in the world must die, suffer or be damaged in his personality," whereas the later suggest: "my own child must be spared, must be protected."

We, too, have observed these two types of moral approaches. One can often witness how professionals working in the field of institutional education, such as physicians, trained or semi-trained medical personnel, teachers or psychologists, take a different view of the state and development of institutional children. Different judgments are made about their needs and behavior than with regard to the children reared in their own family or in their surroundings.

In the last fifty years, countless studies and publications were written, bringing up more and increasingly accurate data relating to the hazards of threatening the physical and mental health of mother-deprived infants and young children reared in institutions. Just as many studies relate to the other side of the picture, stressing the importance of intimate and continuous relationship between mother and child during the process of growth, so that the child may grow into a healthy adult. These two lines, however, intersect but infrequently, both in the the field of research and in practice.

As far as the children reared in residential nurseries are concerned, neither the discovery of hospitalism as such and of the underlying reasons, nor the results of the related psychological research, have improved their conditions.

Whereas the investigations, therapeutic experiences and the conclusions drawn from these as regards education in the family, have grown more and more sophisticated, the efforts directed at promoting the conditions and development of family-deprived, institutionally raised children, have been less successful. Most of the pertinent investigations formulate erroneous conclusions, since the phenomenon itself is not interpreted by them adequately.

Most of the attempts at improvement were based on the assumption of scarcity of stimulation; these claiming that the children live monotonous lives, devoid of impressions and experiences, and have accordingly little opportunity to acquire notions. Some have tried to ease this situation by providing various visual and acoustic stimuli, as for example, by decorating the rooms, relaying music from tape or radio, since the rooms in a family home are also decorated, and the radio is on. Others have tried to improve the environment by hanging toys on the cots, starting as early as the age of birth, or by giving the children certain sensations and teaching them certain notions, according to carefully drawn up schedules.

When discussing the consequences suffered by mother-deprived institutional infants, mention is made of the lack of certain phenomena — in the first place the absence of sensory stimulation transmitted by the mother, also the absence of mother and child playing and learning together, and shortness of time these infants spend in adult company. They try to improve the situation by increasing the number of staff caretakers to reduce the time given to care. Students, part-time undergraduates, other members of the staff of volunteers are enlisted to help in the care-giving operation so that the nurse may devote at least part of her working hours to fondling and petting the babies, to playing with them or to teaching them. Sometimes the petting, playing and teaching is entrusted to auxiliary workers described above. These solutions are resorted to because the caretaker has no spare time to devote to these tasks, if she is to care for 8 to 10 infants in a more or less satisfactory way.

Efforts in this direction can be found in this country too, but literature contains ample reference to the systematic application of these methods (cf. Calkwell, Casler, Damorska, Dennis, Kistiakovskaia, Koch, Manova, Meers, etc.).

Although the actual results expected from systematically allotted or random cuddling, doled out upon instruction, are rather doubtful, the effectiveness of these methods is measured by partial results, and the balance generally appears to be positive. The children do become more cheerful and gay, more open to contact, if compared to either earlier conditions or, as shown by systematic control tests, against control groups. The children's interest may be roused with relative ease; however, they show little spontaneous initiative. If the large number of adults they meet treat them kindly, they come to trust adults, meaning adults in general without distinction, with no special attachment to the one or the other person.

These methods, therefore, have not proved to be efficient in preventing the aberration of personality development described in the paper by Dr. Pikler.

Those who investigated the relationship between subject and caretaker, as well as its effect on the child's development, came somewhat nearer to the mark in finding a real answer to the basic problem.

Various authors, among them Bowlby, note the substantial impairment caused by separation from the mother if there is not adequate maternal substitute. By adequate substitutes most authors understand foster or adoptive mothers, perhaps relatives, like grandmothers, aunts, etc. Institutional education is generally considered to be unsuitable for bringing about a relationship apt to substitute for maternal contact. Only very few authors seem to seek methods for creating, within the institute, conditions under which the infant and young child may find relationships effectively replacing the mother-child relation.

It is, of course, preferable for the infant and young child to live in a family which provides an adequate relationship, for example, to be raised by an affectionate grandmother, to be adopted, etc. In many cases, however, no such solutions can be realized. Accordingly, we have to investigate the problem of whether institutional life necessarily precludes a person-oriented relationship which may serve as a basis for subsequent emotional security.

Relatively little attention has been given to the importance of stability of personal relationships, and to what extend this can be realized. And yet it is common knowledge, almost commonplace in psychological literature, that the supremely important and very rapidly attained developmental achievements of the child can only be organically assimilated in the developing personality, if all the experiences of the child are acquired within a stable system of relationships. Only if everything that happens to the child occurs in the framework of an actual contact, and in an interrelation which enables the child to become aware of the caretaker and of his own self, will the formation of his personal intergrity and of his identity become possible. A stable system of relations is a precondition for the child to live through, without impairment, the frustrations necessary for the maturation of his personality and, this again is a precondition to the child's ability to assimilate the society's pattern of accepted values, its norms, its rules of behavior, its set of prohibitions, by means of imitation, assimilation, and identification. The strength and solidity of a moral basis depends on the depth and strength of the bonds with the person who supplies the pattern, or raises the requirment. If the child lacks a love object, who is a true representative of the moral rules, he will be deprived of being able to identify himself with these demands. Only if such a relation exists, will the institutional child be apt to become a morally and socially self-dependent being.

Yet the dual attitude described by Mead seems to appear here too, for these discoveries are not always applied to institutional children, not even in literature.

Before replying to our earlier question, of whether an institute is at all suitable for providing a stable pattern of relationships, and whether the preconditions for it are available, let us outline the current situation.

Examining the situation in residential nurseries both in Hungary and abroad, as known from literature or from personal experience, the answer must be that these conditions have been scarcely, if at all, realized.

While the absence of consistent personal relationships is mentioned by certain authors, its importance is not estimated properly. Based on the findings of cultural anthropology, and in light of the results of the educational methods of the kibbutzim, some authors believe that, if a fairly large proportion of the children's waking hours are spent in an atmosphere of uniform, affectionate care, development may occur without impairment, even if the adults around him change frequently. Those who have compared these educational conditions with institutional education, however, did not take into account that the requirements for both children and adults in the societies studied in cultural anthropology are different from those prevailing in our family-based modern society. Another fundamentally important fact disregarded by these researchers is that in addition to the caretakers who provide most of the care given to kibbutz-raised children, these children have permanent close relationships with their parents, hence, the parents represent permanence for the children.

Other authors who have investigated the situation and development of institutionally reared infants put the blame for the children's poor emotional reactions, their retarded mental development and the subsequent personality disorders primarily on the recurrent changes of their human environment and the resulting impersonal character of care. Reference is made in this connection to the works of Duhrsen, Du Pan and Roth, Provence and Lipton, Hege and Bischef, Bertove and Dumornd, Meyerhofer and Keller, David and Appell, Timard and Joseph, who have analyzed institutional conditions as well. These works were published in the last 15 years; even the oldest came out almost 20 years later than Anna Freud's report on wartime residential nurseries.

Anna Freud describes the well-known successful attempt to establish stronger relationships between groups of 3-4-5 children. One child assumes the role of the mother figure, or the children designate one chosen adult to substitute in all situations requiring maternal care, and the children insisted on her person, particularly for intimate operations of care. Although the children were in the care of a certain (unspecified) number of adults during the better part of the day, some children would accept warning, criticism or reprimands from that particular person only. It was found that the reactions of the children in these groups very soon turned into the type of emotional reactions commonly experienced in families. Although these reactions increased the difficulties of institutional life by introducing jealousy and the desire to monopolize the beloved person, yet simultaneously with the formation of the children's emotional attachments, they became more difficult to manage but easier to educate.

Rheingold compared the behavior of groups of infants in the care of permanent and changing nurses from the age of 3 months on. No difference was found between the two groups as regards motor development and object-oriented behavior, but from the fifth week on, significantly increasing differences were experienced in the wealth and diversity of the children's vocalization and their social reactions, and mainly in their facial expressions. The author sees the reason for the difference not simply in the absence or presence of a permanent person, but in the fact that a consistent caretaker, who has to look after a few children only, will treat them with more understanding for their behavior and respond to their individual reactions in an increasingly more refined and individual manner, than a caretaker who has to look after different children in turns.

In their investigations focused on the relations between infants and caretakers in a Paris residential nursery, and the amount and content of their interactions, David and Appell recorded the number of nurses who looked after a child during his 10 to 12 weeks spent in the institute. They found that, as a result of days off, paid holidays, night duties, fluctuation of staff, drifting of personnel and probationaries, each child was in the care of 10 to 22 adults, with an average of 16 adults per child. And, yet, in that institute certain efforts towards consistency were made.

Let us review the situation in Hungary.

Since the National Methodological Institute for Residential Nurseries has always set store in building up a consistent person-to-person relationship between child and caretaker, similar emphasis has been put on research, consultation and training in this field on a national level. After a great deal of training in groups as well as individually, and following the 1970 survey, we recorded the monthly breakdown of a caretaker's work in 23 out of the total 46 residential nurseries. Let me add that efforts to achieve consistency in regard to the person of the caretakers are noticeable in practically every institute, and that certain results have been attained. Nevertheless, the present situation is the following:

Investigating a period of one month, among the 261 groups of 32 residential nurseries, we found a single group where only three caretakers had worked; four groups had four caretakers and seven had five. In 150 groups, 6 to 9 caretakers worked in relay, including 52 groups (or 20% of the total number of groups) with nine caretakers taking turns. Nearly 40% of all groups, i.e., 99 groups had been in the care of ten or more caretakers, of these, six groups had seen 17 workers, one had 19 and another group had 21 caretakers; all this within a single month. The situation is aggravated by the fact that in addition to the caretakers figuring in the formal lists, a number of other adults participate in the care of the infants, such as the head matron, aides, students, cleaners, or perhaps the caretaker on duty in the adjacent group, etc.

Of 875 caretakers, only 178 were found to have spent the whole month with one single group, working for at least 18 shifts, but in five institutes not a single caretaker met this requirement, and only one each in three other institutes. On the other hand, 177 caretakers were found to have worked alternating in four or more groups; fifteen nurses worked in six different groups, six in eight groups.

A fairly large number of institutes have achieved a degree of comparative stability with two permanent caretakers assigned to each group. In reality, however, they were occasionally assigned to each other groups as well. Yet even in those institutes it was impossible to have a third permanent substitute stand in for the two so-called permanent nursers. Accordingly, the children have been in the care of varying persons at least twice a week, or 8 to 10 times in a month due to days off, but in actual practice still more often, on account of sick leaves, holidays, night shifts, etc.

The lack of stability is aggravated by the fact that in most institutes the children are from time to time transferred, individually or in groups, from one group into another, quite often into other buildings, which as rule means further changes for the child. Very few institutions have been able to introduce the so-called ascending system, where caretakers move along with the children from one room to another, such moves being often truly unavoidable owing to existing premises.

Taking into account this latter fact as well, a child is in the care of even more caretakers than described during his whole stay in a residential nursery; their number may amount to more than 20 caretakers for a child in over half of the institutes, and in 17 nurseries the children have been in the care of every single caretaker of the institute for shorter or longer periods. From this point of view the smaller institutes are preferable, where the absolute number of caretakers is less, whereas larger institutes may have 50 to 60 nurses.

This situation affects both the nurse and the child. A caretaker who does not usually look after a child will not know the child entrusted to her; a nurse who takes turns in varying groups does not really know any of the children. If she is competent and dedicated, she may get a look from one child, a smile from another, some cooperation from a third child, and peace and quiet in the whole group, but she will not even realize that no real contact has been established with the children. The interactions which may be formed are mostly scanty and stereotyped. She does not know their habits, nor do the children know hers; she is not aware what their crying or gestures mean and is accordingly unable to respond to the needs of the children. Hence, the signs emitted by the children become scarce and increasingly scant, while the caretaker's work gets mechanical, often indifferent.

This is where we come back to the question of whether all this had to be considered an unavoidable institutional impairment. According to our experiences the answer is no. As a condition for the sound emotional, mental and social development of institutionally reared infants and young children, and with a view to their well-structured personality development pattern, we believe that it is possible to evolve intimate, affectionate, stable, continuous relationships between the child and a certain number of specific adults.

While this relationship is meant to replace the mother-child relationship, it differs from it in fundamental characteristics. It has different roots, different motivation, it is composed of different components, and it has a different future.

Any caretaking procedure which would require the caretaker to act in a way resembling the instinctive maternal attitude is dangerous. While the caretaker should increase the person-oriented character of care, she must always be aware that the child she rears is not her own. However emotionally rich she may be, however devoted, she has to remain within the boundaries of her profession. This is necessary for her as well as the child. An overspontaneous relationship, rooted in fervent emotions even if it seems to be occasionally fruitful, evokes uneasiness both in the child and the caretaker. The children develop claims which cannot possibly be satisfied in an institution. A caretaker who arouses emotional expectations and claims which cannot be satisfied, cannot help causing disappointment and painful frustration. She herself will feel uneasy, worried and guilty, both on account of the child she incited to unrealistic claims, and with regard to the other children to whom she has devoted less attention. Her feeling of guilt and concern will often turn into impatience, even aggressiveness. Moreover, the transfer of the child she mothered will leave her emotionally empty and make it difficult for her to turn to other children.

The caretaker, while giving sufficient warmth to all the children in her care, must keep her own feelings in check, lest the children be exposed to the uncontrolled and unrestricted flow of ther emotions. If we want to be successful educators, then, instead of yielding to our instinctive maternal feelings, we have to focus our approach on our interest in the whole process of development of the children; the intensity of feelings must be replaced by the intensity of interest. If the caretaker observes the development of the child with passionate interest, and sees the results of her own work, she will build the basis for a relationship which may offer equal security to all the children in her care.

The most important moments of interaction between child and caretaker are the operations of care. Feeding, cleaning and dressing are the situations most closely resembling family life. The child has the caretaker all to himself. All through infancy and young childhood, the operations of care form the base for person-to-person relationships both in the family and in institutions. If the nurse treats the child from the newborn period with kindness and delicacy, if she prepares the child in advance for what she is going to do and what is going to happen to him, if she gives him continual chances for cooperation, increasing self-dependence, and tries to promote his readiness to perform what he is asked to, then she will give the child a feeling of belonging which is an unparalleled basis for emotional balance.

The first precondition for the nurse's attentive interest is that she must work consistently with the same children. This can be managed if one group is in the care of not more than three caretakers taking turns. Only in this way can the children come to know her, and she to know them. Only if she knows the children well can she look after them, taking increasingly into account their individual needs, only in this way can she guide their education consciously.

The person-oriented character of the relationship is further enhanced, if every nurse of the group has a particular responsiblity for a part of the group. Taking regular notes on the development of the children belonging to her sub-group, she will from time to time size up their state, comportment and development. While she will take care of all the children in the group, she will give a little extra time and extra attention to those in her own sub-group, and the operations of care will take a little longer and will be more playful. The rest of the children will receive this increased attention the next day, or in the next shift, from their special nurse. If the nurse carries this out properly, the children will express by their comportment that they are aware of this primary relation-ship. In her absence they will accept the other nurse assigned to the group, but their relationship will be more intimate with their special nurse.

Our own experience supports the statement that infants and young children who have increased ties with one particular adult are indeed more difficult to manage. They gambol during care, they are playful and romping, keep on insisting on doing or having something, or refusing it. They are hurt when things turn out differently, they are insistent and jealous; in other words, they resemble the family-reared children in their attitudes.

In order that a nurse may devote all her attention and interest to the child during care, the other children must make this possible for her. That is, they must be able to spend their waking hours outside the operations of care in happy activity, they must have a chance for playing and romping as they please. It is particularly important for institutionally reared infants to be able to convert their energies into happy, self-dependent activity from the youngest age on, as continuously as possible. The adult who looks after a number of children, can devote relatively little time to direct attention to a particular child. Particularly under institutional conditions, continually growing and varied activity is rooted primarily in the children's self-initiated activity, the results of which will stimulate them to further activity.

In the almost thirty years of our Institute's work we have been intent on evolving stable, person-oriented relationships of the children along these lines, thus preparing the children for evolving later secure and lasting relationships, formulating independent opinions and adapting to society.

We cannot, of course, reply to the question of whether children from our Institute have all turned into harmonious personalitites, whether they are happy and balanced, and can cope with all their individual problems. However, our follow-up studies sponsored by the WHO indicate that children from our Institute have made good adjustments to society. Their level of schooling shows no detrimental difference when compared with their age group; they show neither vagrancy nor delinquency.

Five of the girls have given birth to children, all in marriage, under normal family conditions, and in spite of their institutional background, they have so far proved to be competent parents.

REFERENCES

Bertoye, P. amd C. Dumorand, "Troubles de croissance du nourisson par choc affectif," Rev. Hyg. Med. Soc., 1957, 5, 187.

Biermann, G., "Kinder in Ysrael," Praxis der Kinderpsychol. und Kinderpsychiatrie, 1967, 16, 97.

Bowlby, J., Maternal Care and Mental Health, WHO, Geneva, 1951.

Burlingame, D. and A. Freud, Infants Without Families, London: G. Allen and Unwin Ltd, 1943.

Caldwell, M.B. and J.B. Richmond, The Children's Center in Syracuse, New York. Early Child Care, New York: Atherton Press, 1968.

Casler, L., "The Effects of Extra Stimulation on a Group of Institutionalized Children," Genet. Psychol. Monogr, 1965, 71, 137.

Damborska, M., "Erziehungsproblemen beim Saugling und Kleinkind Monatskurse," f.d. Aerztl. Fortbildung, 1967, 17, 212.

David, M. and G. Appell, "Etude des facteurs de carence affective dans une pouponniere," Psychiatrie de l'Enfant, 1962, 4, 407.

Dennis, W. and Y. Sayegh, "The Effects of Supplementary Experience upon the Behavioral Development of Infants in Institution," Child Dev, 1965, 36, 81.

De Wit, J., "Some Critical Remarks on Maternal Deprivation," Acta Paedopsychiatrica, 1964, 31, 240.

Du Pan, R.M. and S. Roth, "The Psychological Development of a Group of Children Brought up in a Hospital-type Resident Nursery," J. Pediat, 1955, 47, 124.

Duhrssen, A., Heimkinder und Pflegekinder in ihrer Entwicklung, Verl. Medizinische Psychol., Gottingen, 1969.

Falk, J. and E. Pikler, "Data to the Social Adjustment of Children Reared in our Institute," Magyar Pszichologiai Szemle, 1972, 29, 488-500. (text in Hungarian).

Koch, J., "Die psychische Entwicklung und Erziehung der Kinder im Sauglingsheim," Z. arztl. Fortbild, 1960, 54, 1109.

Manova-Tomova, V., "Neuropsychiache Entwicklung und Erziehung der Kinder im Alter von O bis 3 Jahren," Die Heilberufe, 1961, 14, 6.

Marcus, J., "Early Child Development in Kibbutz Group Care," Early Child Development and Care, 1971, 1, 67.

Mead, M., La carence maternelle du point de vue de l'anthropoligie culturelle. La carence de soins maternels. OMS, Geneve, 1962, 44.

Meyerhofer, M., and W. Keller, Frustration im fruhen Kindesalter, H. Huber Verl. Bern., 1966.

Provence, S. and R. Lipton, Infants in Institution. Internat. Univ. Press, New York, 1962.

Rheingold, H.L., "The Modificationof Social Responsiveness in Institutional Babies," Monogr. Soc. Res. Child Development, 1956, 21, No. 23.

Schmalchr, F., Fruhe Mutterentbegrung bei Mensch und Tier Ernst Reinhardt Verl. Munchen/Basel, 1968

Tizard, B. and A. Joseph, "Cognitive Development of Young Children in Residential Care," J. Child Psychol. Psychiat, 1970, 11, 177.

FEEDINGS AS ONE OF THE MAIN SCENES OF THE ADULT-CHILD RELATION- SHIP

Maria Vincze, M.D.

In our time, children do not have to die in residential nursery homes anymore. However, we are still a far cry from residential nurseries which offer a real home for cheerful active children.

Mehringer wrote in 1966: "I find it alarming how little one knows about the life of nursery home children. But those who know of their nightmare conditions cannot forget the sight of lonely infants in aligned rows of cribs, waiting in vain for someone to approach them with that vital element, love; feeding lines, cleaning lines, potty lines, babies clamped between the nurse's knees, with the food shoveled in their mouths at routine speed, heads averted. None of the adults finds the time to take each one in his arms, to feed him leisurely, to laugh with him; or to clean him, feed him, and put him to bed so that both of them enjoy it;...Who would believe," asks Mehringer, "that in nursery homes we are still faced with that sight?"

Mehringer is not alone with his nightmarish experiences. The similarity of the situation the world over is uncanny. While the practice of family rearing shows remarkable divergencies even in modern societies, the poor practices of care in nursery homes are often so much alike it is as if the caretakers of USA institutes had studied in Hungarian nursery homes, and the Hungarian attendants seem to have copied Swiss methods.

Since my paper is focused on feeding, let us quote Provence and Lipton in regard to the feeding methods used in American nursery homes:

"Feedings for the youngest infants (0 to 4 months) were given every four hours, six times daily. Feeding times were fixed according to the institution's routine, and there was little chance for modification to meet an indivdual infant's needs. If a baby was crying when the attendant began to prepare the group, he might receive his bottle first; if he was asleep, he was awakened to eat. Prior to feedings, each infant was diapered and returned to his crib where he was placed on his side with a blanket roll at the back to prevent rolling. The nipple was placed in his mouth and the bottle propped on a small pillow. The attendant worked quickly in order that the other seven to nine infants could be fed...The youngest institutionalized infants lost the nipple frequently, and its return and their continued sucking were entirely dependent on the attendant. If she was watchful and not otherwise occupied, or if the baby cried loudly enough to get her attention, the nipple might be returned promptly. More often the nipple was returned after some delay...During feeding the institutionalized infant experienced virtually no change in the quality or quantity of outside stimulation except for the presence of the nipple in the mouth...The infant who is held for feedings by his mother has an enormously different experience and set of sensations. As he is picked up and held, his body position is changed radically from lying on his back or abdomen;...he experiences a human contact, a social interchange with all the variety of both positive and negative emotions. The experience of being fed in an emotionally enriched environment is a point of major difference from

from the insitutional procedure...At mealtimes the practice was to feed each infant in his crib lying on his back. After about 18 months he was usually allowed to sit up in a corner of his crib for meals. The bowl was held close to the infants' face and the food quickly and efficiently spooned into his mouth. While the infant was not actively restrained, any attempts he made to move about for whatever reason were discouraged by the attendant's words, tone of voice, and facial expression. The children were almost unbelievably inactive during this process, only rarely attempting to touch the spoon, bowl, or attendant, although they watched her face attentively. The attendant was usually pleasant in her ministrations in the few minutes while she prepared a baby for feeding and removed his bib afterward, but the interchange during the entire period was minimal. The staff seemed to believe that such social interchange would prolong the time required to feed by exciting the babies and making them "uncooperative." They more often talked to each other than to the babies they were feeding."

Speaking of Swiss nursery homes, Meyerhofer and Keller describe their experiences in 1966 as follows:

"Spoon-fed children as a rule swallow the food without resistance and without apparent enjoyment. But in each group a child will protest by shutting his lips tightly, by turning away his head or trunk, or by crying — not using his arms or hands, because these are pinned to his sides —; he turns the food in his mouth, and ejects it as soon as he can. Feedings are performed everywhere in identical situations: the child is half lying in the nurse's lap, his right arm pinned down to the trunk of the nurse, his left hand held down by the nurse's left hand. Hence, the infant cannot touch the spoon. Infants aged one or two years are placed on a chair, bench, pot or pot-bench for feedings. The nurse sits opposite, holds the bowl at mouth level, carefully watching the child, lest he touch the bowl. While she feeds one child, the others are waiting. The children are fed by alternating relays or attendants everywhere. The aim is the same in all homes: get done with feeding in the shortest possible time. Sequence of feeding: as a rule the first bowl goes to the child who cries loudest, sometimes to the nurse's favorite. But when they try to train the children to be patient, the one most anxious to eat will have to wait the longest. Quite often, children aged 18-24 months get the same food as the adults, sitting at inconveniently high tables. They are made to sit at the table and wait for their meals, at times for 20 minutes. The children get bored and quarrelsome; some are tied to their chairs."

Our own observations relate to the meals of some 1500 children in 135 groups of 32 nursery homes, from September 1971 to September 1973.

Compared with the feeding habit in US and Swiss nursery homes described above, we can speak of a certain favorable difference in Hungary. Here the children are invariably picked up for feeding, and we never saw a child tied to a chair.

Yet the common characteristics are prevalent. In most of the nursery homes joyless babies are fed joylessly by dreary adults. The caretakers vary incessantly, and to finish the main meal as soon as possible, the nurse on morning duty combines forces with the one on afternoon duty, and still further forces are enlisted. The children are not told when their turn will come, they have to wait now more, then less; they don't care who feeds them, at what rate and with what method; one nurse will start with the most fractious child, the other with the most fretful, the third with her favorite, while the fourth nurse makes the most eager one wait longest "so that he learns to wait for his turn." The caretakers do not expect the child to cooperate, nor do they pay attention to the child's signals; the child's activity is restrained by widely varying means. Immobilizing both his arms with obvious or disguised methods, they shove the food mechanically or stuff it roughly in his mouth from a bowl held close to his chin; the averted head of the child is grabbed and turned back; quite often the child is placed on a raised chair or bench, but even so his mouth will hardly reach the level of the table.

In the majority of nursery homes, therefore, the characteristic features of feeding are:

> Impersonality
> Haste, hurry-scurry, disorganization
> The children's enforced passivity
> Ignoring the signals emitted by the children
> A generally low-spirited atmosphere during meals

These traits are interdependent; one gives rise to the other.

Let us describe a case observed in detail:

A group of fourteen infants around 18 months of age in a residential nursery are fed by six adults: two caretakers from the morning shifts, two from the afternoon shift, the cleaning woman, and a caretaker from the neighboring group. The adults rush around the children; at one time one enters and picks up a child to feed him, at another time someone else feeds him. At one moment two adults feed the babies, at another six. The children are not given any information. The nurses enter and leave the room in silence. The children hustle around the nurses who are feeding, they cry, pull each other's hair, pull at the nurse who is feeding a child. The most vexing one if picked up as a rule, he gets a bib and is being fed. Towards the end of a feeding time the caretakers ask each other again and again: who hasn't eaten yet? And since six nurses did the feeding coming and going, appearing and disappearing, the observer is ultimately not sure at all whether one of the children has not been fed twice, or left out. The child is not called up, he is not told that it's his turn and what he is going to have; conversation with the children is limited to "eat it up, there's a good boy" and "it's nice." The child is put down while the nurse prepares for the next course, but no one tells the child why he is put down during meals.

Children who got their food and drink are also dismissed without a word. Three of them — Attila aged 18 months, Ila aged 19 months and Sanyika aged 20 months — promptly lie down on the floor after feeding, they whimper and wail for some 20 to 30 minutes. The nurses' "stop crying Attila" or "get up from the floor Sanyika" sound unconvincing. The feeding technique is not uniform: some nurses will reach out with their left arm over the child's left shoulder, pressing it down, and put the bowl close under his chin; others place their arms under his left armpit, so that the child's shoulder is raised to immobilization; we have also seen a nurse who, unable to get on with the feeding, placed the child in the chair, and tried to force the food upon him in that position. The question of the child's activity does not even come up. The children do not even try to get hold of the spoon or the cake. Even the beaker of tea is lifted to their mouths by the nurse. Although most of the children are apparently waiting for their turn, all of them (with the exception of a single good eater) lost interest by the time their turn came; some of them were disgusted. The nurses shovelled a large spoonful of vegetable in the baby's mouth, which was followed by the next spoonful, not waiting for the child to swallow the first, until he was ready to throw it up. After this uncomfortable procedure of feeding, one of the children, while being fed the cake, vomited the whole meal; the nurse, sorry for her soiled dress, kept her temper with considerable self control, apparently on account of the visitor's presence, so as not to scold the child.

Sure, the example just described is strikingly bad, but not exceptional; we could relate the case of another nursery home, where the nurse kept shouting at the group of 18 to 24 month olds during the whole meal. Of the 187 sentences recorded, only 30 contained indifferent orders, 128 were "don'ts." Or I might speak of the various methods ostensibly aimed at training the children "to eat by themselves." In one of the homes we visited, this was done in the following way: the children aged 13 to 15 months, were put on chairs, placed close to the table. The nurse, standing behind the back of the children and not waiting till the baby made an attempt to eat, put his hand on the spoon and raised the spoon into the mouth of the child, whether he wanted to eat or not; into the bargain, the nurse grabbed the child's head from behind to prevent him from turning away. In another home, the training to self-dependence of children aged 18 to 24 months means that instead of taking the child in the nurse's lap, he was seated on a chair facing the nurse. During the feeding operation the children's arms were dangling inertly by their sides; neither made the least attempt to reach for the bowl or spoon.

Brute force is often replaced by indifferent routine, outright banning of activity by covert methods; military commands may merge into impersonal, mawkish pleasantness.

When compared with what we had seen two years ago, improvement could be recorded in a number of homes. The National Methodological Institute continually arranges one-week refresher courses for the matrons and caretakers of nursery homes; these are primarily responsible for the serious efforts witnessed in improving the methods of care. In some institutes, feeding and cleaning lines have been eliminated, and continuous care has been introduced. We have seen a meal of a group of older children eating happily, with the children permitted to serve themselves from the dish; they ate alone and neatly, while the caretakers gave patient assistance to those who could not get on. We saw nurses who waited for the child to slacken or open his mouth for the spoon; some who did tried to promote the child's activity by placing his hand on the cup and clasping it. We met more than one nurse who talked to the child in a kind tone but only rarely met children who responded to the nurse's initiative, or who initiated a contact. Not a single one of the 1500 children behaved like a child of similar age does at home during feedings or during the preparations.

And yet it is possible to evolve a relationship in institutional conditions during the operations of care. Feedings are of primary importance in building a relationship, even though during feedings the contact is not spectacular, since there is but little talk or smiling. And yet it is a critically important situation, not only because the meals are of vital importance in the life of a young child or because eating is a great source of pleasure, but also because the adult's response to he child's small signals establishes his confidence in the adult, which is the basis of contact.

This is true in the family as well. Although by the end of the first year for most infants feedings are not the most important mother-interaction anymore, he will have learned that he is able to influence his mother's comportment by his own actions, and this is an experience which begins to form right in the first weeks and which appears to determine the nature of the child's attachment.

Ainsworth and Bell investigated the quality and formation of the mother-infant attachment, and the degree of attachment considering different maternal attitudes. This was done in a longitudinal study based on extensive observations. It was found that the manner of care of those mothers who were able to look at things from the point of view of the infant, led to harmonious interactions, not only in the feeding situation, but in all other situations. With regard to the feeding methods, it was found that irrespective of whether feedings occurred on a self-demand basis, or in a more formal system, any method is appropriate which satisfies the infant, which regulates his rhythm, and which allows him to partake actively in the meal, instead of accepting it passively. For facilitating an early patterning of rhythm, it appears to be important that the infant be able to initiate feeding and to determine the amount of his food intake; active participation in the timing and rate of the meals seems to promote a mutually satisfactory mother-infant interaction. Based on these findings, the authors set up the following hypothesis: the favorable feedback to the various signals, actions and communications of the infant permit him to have confidence in his capacity to influence the events happening to him, and this sensation of effectiveness leads to a feeling of competence.

Although Ainsworth et al. and many others have emphatically stressed the paramount importance of feedings in the patterning of interaction, yet we believe, like Peter Wolff, another researcher of the infant-child relationship, that the mother has a chance for compensation, even if she has made mistakes in the feeding situation.

The situation is different in an institute. There is no method of compensation, rectification, correction. Here feedings are indeed a primary instrument of building up relationships, even though institutes do not provide the ideal conditions for feeding.

It is impossible, for example, to realize the self-demand system since the attendants cannot feed every child at the moment he prefers. On the other hand, it is possible not to pick the children up at random, following the attendant's whim, at the same time exposing the child to the impatience and wailing of his peers. It is possible to put into practice an order of feeding in which every child will be aware of his place.

It is likewise impossible in an institute to have each child consistently fed by one and the same adult: but it is possible to have three attendants alternate. And the child may justly expect these three stable attendants:

To hold him in their laps in a similar way;

To offer him the spoon or cup in an identical manner;

To feed him at a uniform rate following the rhythm indicated by the child;

To stop feeding at the slightest indication, to feed him not a mouthful more than he wants to have;

That "his" three attendants understand and take into consideration the temperature and thickness of food he prefers;

That "his" three attendants promote and enjoy each and every manifestation of his activity, such as:

Slacking his mouth when touched by the spoon, and later opening it when viewing the spoon; not to hurry meals so that he may do this;

Taking the bowl in his hands and tilting it himself; to be able to do so, he must be held from the very beginning so that the can move both arms freely;

Sitting at the table himself, and making attempts at self-dependent eating with the aid of the attendant;

He may further expect to sit at the table as comfortably as the adult, without his feet dangling and his chin touching the table, and be given food appropriate for his degree of maturity.

We believe that satisfying all these claims is possible and necessary to achieve a sound caretaker-infant relationship, since all these must be fulfilled so that the child may realize his own effectiveness, which in turn will result in a feeling of competence.

The danger of poor feeding methods is not that the children lose their appetite or become greedy. The meals represent one of the situations where interactions may suffer, and the hazard is in the potential impact on the child's whole personality.

We are justified in being worried about the future of the child. We must seek a solution right now, not only in order to eliminate our worry about the future, but also because the effort must be directed both at improving our methods of care and in striving to evolve person-oriented relationships.

Ainsworth, S.and S.M. Bell, <u>Some Contemporary Patterns of Mother-Infant Interaction in the Feeding Situation: Stimulation in Early Infancy</u>, Academic Press, 1969, 133-171.

Mehringer, A., "Geschutzte Kleinkinderzeit," <u>Unsere Jugend</u>, 1966, 18, Heft 5.

Meyerhofer, M. and W. Keller, <u>Frustration im fruhen Kindersalter</u>, H. Huber Verl, Bern, 1966.

Provence, S. and R. Lipton, <u>Infants in Institution</u>, Internat. Univ. Press, New York, 1962.

Wolff, P.H., "The Natural History of a Family," <u>Determinants of Infant Behavior II</u>, Methuen, 1963, 139-171.

POSTSCRIPT

In this manual many of the articles refer to the Demonstration Infant Program in Palo Alto which operated from 1972-1979. RIE activities are now directed by Magda Gerber and RIE Board of Directors at **Resources for Infant Educarers**, 1550 Murray Circle, Los Angeles, CA 90026 (213/663-5330).

At the RIE Center we offer classes for:

- **Expectant Parents** - How to prepare for the baby, the home environment, the family's changing needs, dealing with emotions (fears, hopes, moods, etc.) expectations and reality.

- **Parent-Infant Guidance Classes** - What parents can realistically 'expect' of their babies at any given stage of development, how to establish healthy patterns of behavior from the beginning, how to set up infant oriented environments in the home, how to respond to difficult behavior such as crying, how to observe, understand, respect and enjoy the individuality of each baby.

- **RIE I Certification Training** which includes an overview of the RIE philosophy, gross motor, fine motor and social-emotional development of the infant, designing the environment, planning curricula, issues in parenting and observational skills.

  Graduates of RIE I basic training may enroll in **RIE II** practicum where they learn to demonstrate the RIE approach with parents and infants in RIE's parent-infant guidance classes. Upon the successful completion of RIE II, students may apply for acceptance in the **RIE III** Supervised Teaching and Evaluation program. As Interns, RIE III must be completed three times in order to be considered for a **RIE Associate** diploma to be awarded.

For parents and professionals not from the Los Angeles area, each year RIE also offers two-week intensives, one in the summer and one in the winter. Please contact the RIE office for information on dates and times of classes.

APPENDICES

Dear Parent

Caring For Infants With Respect

Magda Gerber

In *Dear Parent*, infant specialist Magda Gerber shares her life work with parents and professionals. A helpful and reassuring resource for parents and caregivers of new babies and growing infants, the book includes her vision, wisdom and practical guidance about such topics as:

- **What do infants need? And what do parents need?**

- **How parents can provide an environment in which both they and their infants thrive.**

- **The motor skills and coping skills your baby can learn best from his own inner resources from birth.**

- **The social, emotional and language skills your baby can learn best with your help.**

- **The importance of talking and listening to your baby.**

- **How Magda's respectful "Educaring" differs from other approaches.**

EDITED BY JOAN WEAVER

A PUBLICATION OF

Resources for Infant Educarers

DEAR PARENT • ISBN # 1-892560-01-1 • $14.95 US/$20.95 CAN

APPENDIX B

WITH CARE AND RESPECT

•

A Video Series

A thoughtful, consistent and rewarding approach to infant care for parents, professionals, and students.

---

1. ON THEIR OWN/ WITH OUR HELP

(Examples of Selective Intervention)

As several babies freely explore a playroom, infant specialist Magda Gerber shows when NOT to interfere with their choices and solutions. When she does offer help, she involves the infant's active participation.

2. THE WAY WE SEE THEM

(Learning to Observe Infants)

Watching infants interact and engage in self-teaching, viewers learn first hand the values of careful observation. Commentary by Dr. Thomas Forrest helps us appreciate the infants' resourcefulness, tolerance of frustration and individual learning styles.

These videos, originally produced as films by The National Commission on Resources for Youth, Inc, reflect the philosophy of Resources for Infant Educarers and its founders, Thomas Forrest, M.D., pediatric neurologist Children's Health Council, Palo Alto, CA and Magda Gerber, infant specialist, Pacific Oaks College, Pasadena, CA.

---

available from the RIE office:

PURCHASE PRICE $50 EACH

Shipping and handling costs $3.00 per video plus .0825% tax for California residents.

If you are a parent or a professional involved in the day-to-day caring and educating of infants and young children, RIE has resources to offer you. Our goal is to improve the quality of infant care in any setting: home, hospital, day care facility, parent-infant groups.

In order to foster quality care RIE encourages:

• **Basic trust** in the child to be an initiator, an explorer and a self learner.

• An **environment** for the child that is physically safe, cognitively challenging and emotionally nurturing.

• Time for **uninterrupted play**.

• **Freedom to explore** and interact with other infants.

• Involvement of the child in all care activities to allow the child to become an **active participant** rather than a passive recipient.

• **Sensitive observation** of the child in order to understand his and her needs

.• **Consistency**, clearly defined limits and expectations to develop discipline

Respect is the Guideline of RIE's Philosophy. The Educarer shows respect, for example, by not picking up an infant without telling him beforehand, by talking directly to him and not over him and by waiting for the child's response.

RIE'S GOAL IS TO HELP RAISE AUTHENTIC INFANTS WHO ARE:

COMPETENT	*CONFIDENT*
CURIOUS	*ATTENTIVE*
EXPLORING	*COOPERATIVE*
SECURE	*PEACEFUL*
FOCUSED	*SELF-INITIATING*
RESOURCEFUL	*INVOLVED*
CHEERFUL	*AWARE*
INTERESTED	*and* *INNER-DIRECTED*

THE RIE APPROACH

RIE's unique philosophy and methodology in working with infants was developed in the United States by educator and infant specialist Magda Gerber, built on the work of Hungarian pediatrician, Emmi Pikler, M.D. This approach was first demonstrated betwen 1972 and 1977 in the United States at the Demonstration Infant Program in Palo Alto, California through the Children's Health Council by Magda Gerber and pediatric neurologist Tom Forrest, M.D. In order to continue educating parents and professionals in their approach, they founded Resources for Infant Educarers (RIE) as a non-profit corporation in 1978 in Los Angeles, California with Magda Gerber as the Founding Director. RIE offers classes in observation and guidance for parents who bring their infants to class, and also courses for professionals, as well as a variety of other services. Contact RIE for trained Associates who, having completed the three-part training plus further requirements, are certified to teach either RIE parent/infant classes or RIE professional courses.

RESOURCES FOR INFANT EDUCARERS
OFFERS TO PARENTS AND EXPECTANT PARENTS:

Parent-Infant Observation and Guidance Classes in parent-infant communication and understanding of your needs and baby's needs;

Classes on how to prepare for a good beginning;

Dear Parent, a reassuring book written by Magda Gerber with pracical ideas and suggestions on how to care respectfully for your baby;

Suggestions for planning your baby's environment (space and objects);

Home assistance for healthy newborns, as well as for infants at risk;

Availability of literature, films, discussions, and parent-support groups;

Manual of the RIE philosophy with practical suggestions for parents;

Quarterly newsletter for RIE members.

AND FOR THE PROFESSIONAL...

A certified training program in the RIE philosophy and its implementation;

Assistance in design and set-up of child care centers;

Curriculum development;

Assistance to programs for infants with at-risk conditions;

In-service staff training;

Workshops;

Consulting services;

Manual of the RIE philosophy and its applications;

Audio-visual materials specifically developed to demonstrate RIE's philosophy in action

Quarterly newsletter for RIE members.

RIE is a non-profit organization dependent upon fees, grants and contributions to fund its efforts. Fees for services depend upon need and ability to pay.

"SEEING INFANTS WITH NEW EYES"

A half-hour videodocumentary that combines a portrait of infant specialist Magda Gerber with a presentation of her unique philosophy on raising autonomous infants. Narrated by Ned Beatty.

For further information, please call **RIE**: (323) 663-5330

"Seeing Infants With New Eyes" can be ordered for purchase from:
Resources for Infant Educarers
1550 Murray Circle
Los Angeles, CA 90026

PURCHASE COST: $55 for RIE members, $65 for others
Priority mail postage charge:$3.00 for up to two videos in same envelope plus .0825% tax for California residents

---

"SEE HOW THEY MOVE"

The first of the three-part series "Infants at RIE," this video presents natural gross motor development of infants and toddlers and is available for purchase. "See How They Play," and a third whose title will be announced are in production and will cover manipulation, play, interaction and social-emotional development.

PURCHASECOST: $65 for RIE members, $75 for others
Priority mail postage charge: $3.00 for up to two videos in same envelope plus .0825% tax for California residents

YOU CAN BECOME A MEMBER OF RIE

As a RIE member you will receive:
• quarterly issues of *Educaring*;
• discounts on all class offerings;
• discounts on the RIE Manual (philosophy and practical suggestions);
• discounts on purchase and rental of some RIE audio-visual materials;
• discounts on fees for RIE-sponsored conferences, workshops, lectures, and other special events.

As a member you can actively participate and vote at yearly membership meetings.

RIE MEMBERSHIP REGISTRATION FORM
Membership Year July 1 to June 30

Name: _____

Address: _____

City/State/Zip: _____

Phone Numbers:(   ) _____ work (   ) _____ home

Occupation: _____

Check one:
❏ Parent   ❏ Student   ❏ Professional   ❏ Other
I wish to join RIE as a new member in the following category:
Basic $40 ___   Organizational $50 ___
Supporting $50 ___   Sustaining Org. $100 ___
Sustaining $75 ___   (receive two issues of *Educaring*)
Student $20 ___

You may also use this form to order RIE materials; please add .0825% sales tax for California residents. <u>Postage add $3.00 per Manual and $3.00 for up to two videos in same envelope.</u>

• **RIE Manuals** $12 member price; $16 non-member
Please send ____ Manuals at $____ each $_____

• **Sets of 18 past issues of *Educaring*** $25.50

Please send ____ *Educaring* Sets (postage included) $_____

Total including postage enclosed (may include membership & materials), payable in United States currency, to RIE:

$_____

Send remittance to: **RIE** • 1550 Murray Circle, Los Angeles, CA 90026

YOU CAN BECOME A MEMBER OF RIE

As a RIE member you will receive:
• quarterly issues of *Educaring*;
• discounts on all class offerings;
• discounts on the RIE Manual (philosophy and practical suggestions);
• discounts on purchase and rental of some RIE audio-visual materials;
• discounts on fees for RIE-sponsored conferences, workshops, lectures, and other special events.

As a member you can actively participate and vote at yearly membership meetings.

RIE MEMBERSHIP REGISTRATION FORM
Membership Year July 1 to June 30

Name: _____

Address: _____

City/State/Zip: _____

Phone Numbers:( ) _____ work ( ) _____ home

Occupation: _____

Check one:
❑ Parent   ❑ Student   ❑ Professional   ❑ Other
I wish to join RIE as a new member in the following category:
Basic $40 ___   Organizational $50 ___
Supporting $50 ___   Sustaining Org. $100 ___
Sustaining $75 ___   (receive two issues of *Educaring*)
Student $20 ___

You may also use this form to order RIE materials; please add .0825% sales tax for California residents. Postage add $3.00 per Manual and $3.00 for up to two videos in same envelope.

• **RIE Manuals** $12 member price; $16 non-member
Please send ___ Manuals at $___ each $_____

• **Sets of 18 past issues of *Educaring*** $25.50

Please send ___ *Educaring* Sets (postage included) $_____

Total including postage enclosed (may include membership & materials), payable in United States currency, to RIE:
$_____

Send remittance to: ***RIE*** • 1550 Murray Circle, Los Angeles, CA 90026